Simple Gifts:
Living a Spirited Life

Tobie Hewitt

CreateSpace
Spiral Path Press
Copyright © 2012 Tobie Hewitt
All rights reserved.
ISBN-10: 1479108413
ISBN-13: 978-1479108411

My deepest thanks to the following people who in one way or another encouraged me on this path:

Patti Borrelli, William Claire,
Char Hacker, and Barbara Lelyveld

Dedicated to:
Alex and Jane;
Roger, who has always been there;
and
William

Special thanks, with love, to Jane Elyse Ives
for the cover illustration

"We are not human beings having a spiritual experience. We are spiritual beings having a human experience" (Pierre Teilhard de Chardin).

Table of Contents

Chapter 1: The Gift of Wonder:
First Encounters with Spirit 1

Chapter 2: The Gift of Knowledge:
Who and What are Spirits, Ghosts, and Entities.......18

Chapter 3: The Gift of Counsel:
First Readings 38

Chapter 4: The Gift of Communication:
Serving as a Conduit 52

Chapter 5: The Gift of Healing:
Helping to Salve the Spirit 71

Chapter 6: The Gift of Knowing:
Developing and Using Intuition 92

Chapter 7: The Gift of Miracles:
It's Not Just a Coincidence 107

Chapter 8: The Gift of Empathy:
Caring Enough to Receive 122

Chapter 9: The Gift of Discernment:
Forays into Religion 133

Chapter 10: The Gift of Community:
Building Spiritual Community 142

Chapter 1

The Gift of Wonder:
First Encounters with Spirit

*To see a World in a grain of sand
And a Heaven in a wild flower,
Hold infinity in the palm of your hand
And eternity in an hour.
(William Blake)*

The first time I encountered the "lightening and brightening," I must have been about 4-years old. It was a warm spring day, after the final traces of dirt-tinged snow had melted and the crocuses were in their last days of bloom. Surrounded by a white picket fence, I was playing alone in the backyard of my parents' home in Schenectady, New York. My brand new swing set stood in one corner. The height of the steps leading up to the slide was intimidating to say the least and it always felt as though I was climbing a tall mountain when I tried to reach the top. I knew my mother could see me from inside her bedroom window as she finished folding clothes, arranging these in piles on her white chenille bedspread. One old pine towered over me, and a forsythia bush was in full bloom in a corner of the yard. On the other side of the fence, maples cast a small amount of shade towards me. Opposite the swing set there was a garden where the bulb flowers grew in groups—the variously colored tulips, the hyacinths spreading their purple fragrance, a sunny halo of daffodils, and, of course, the crocuses lining the edges of the garden.

As I lay on my back on the soft spring grass, suddenly the blueness of the sky seemed to intensify, and the clouds whitened and began to glow on the sea of deepening azure. I recall being startled by the sudden shift, and sat up to look around me. I checked to see if my mother was still visible through the window, but she wasn't. I looked at the grass around me. Each blade seemed to stand apart from its neighbor, shimmering and releasing a powerful, though delicious smell of earth and, for lack of a better description, what green would smell like on a spring day if green and not grass were the usual fragrance one could detect.

I sat perfectly still, serenely exhilarated by this new manner of experiencing my familiar backyard. My skin seemed to be caressed by the air, held warmly like a swaddled baby in its mother's arms. I could not move, but I felt safe and strangely loved as though someone was hugging me. The flowers in the garden also seemed to emit an aura of intense and vibrant colors as though the colors and not the flowers were expanding into the shimmering air. From above me, I could suddenly hear a sound I had never heard before, a tinkling twinkling sound like tiny wind chimes. I realized that the pine needles were somehow spraying this sound down upon me like a golden vapor. As this mist and sound reached me, it lingered in mid-air for a moment and then disappeared like rain into the ground.

A golden aura clung to everything around me, brightening the already vibrant and vibrating colors. I stayed immobile as the passionate hues, smells, and sounds grew to a harmonic crescendo of expression until with one final burst the world around me returned to normal. The grass lay again as grass and the pine was just pine. The flowers waved in the soft breeze as flowers do every day and the clouds once more clung softly to a blue sky. I shuddered and blinked rapidly, saddened by this return to the ordinary.

I never knew what had triggered that first episode, but from then on, periodically there were instances of intense sensory perception of my environment. As a child, I enjoyed these moments and somehow believed them to be common occurrences that everyone encountered. As I grew older, I came to realize that no one else around me perceived this wondrous shift in reality. These moments of synesthesia didn't happen more than a couple times a year and felt like a gift for good behavior more than anything else. They seemed to happen more often than not in natural settings, but sometimes, amidst the chaotic tensions of the city, I would experience a pocket of serenity and solitude that included the "lightening and brightening" as I called these moments. Then, the pavement would shimmer and the blue sky would reflect forever in the facing glass panes of the buildings. Then, the people around me would glow and sparks of golden and silver light would spin out from their bodies. In this moment of frozen space and time, I could not feel beyond the heightened awareness of my senses, could not detect any pain or sorrow or negative thoughts coming into me from those around me. Instead, I was filled with an overwhelming sense of joy and happiness. It was the sensation of entering a painting and being able to squish the paint through my fingers, or entering a piece of music and having each note caress my inner being.

It was not until quite recently that I found out that other people did, or at least had, encountered these golden moments of joy and wonder. I learned that one name for the phenomenon was *Shekinah* and was a visible expression of a divine presence. By any name, the phenomenon felt both joyful and holy, and I knew that I was very fortunate to be allowed to experience such wonderful sensations.

Whether surrounded by nature or architecture, I felt blessed by these moments of respite and I would bask and relax as though I was on vacation on a warm and sunny beach. I would breathe deeply, and feel myself a part of a wider and more brilliant reality, comforted by the idea that apparently there was a place or a state of existence in which I belonged, where I didn't need to apologetically excuse myself from the simple pleasures that other people around me seemed to enjoy. I ventured to hope that someday I might feel this sense of peace at will and gain a measure of control over entering this calm and gentle space.

One day, as I entered my backyard, I noticed a man sitting on the edge of the wooden sandbox my father had constructed for me. On either side of the sandpit there were wide planks of wood on which my friends and I could sit and play without getting too messy. I was surprised when I saw the man sitting on one of the planks. It was a thin, old man dressed somewhat dapperly in brown pants and a brown vest with a light tan button-down shirt underneath. He wore a hat and supported himself on a cane he held between his bent legs.

I had been carefully taught not to speak to strangers and so I ran out of the gate and to the side door of my house. I called to my mother, who was cooking lunch in our knotty pine-paneled kitchen. As she came to the door, I exclaimed that there was a man sitting in my sandbox. She came running down the steps and around to the backyard. There was no one in the yard at all.

"What are you talking about?" she asked exasperated at having been interrupted from her work.

"There was an old man sitting there." I pointed to the spot on the side of the sandbox where the man had been just moments before.

"Well," she said patiently, "It must have been Betsy's grandfather from down the street. I hear he gets disoriented and wanders away. But look, he's gone now. Just go back to playing and we'll have lunch soon."

My mother turned and went back inside the house and I stood there thoroughly perplexed. I may have been young at the time, but I was fairly certain that the man I had seen could not have somehow vaulted our fence and taken off past the far side of the house. If he had come out the gate, he would have passed me. Instead, the man was simply gone. I wondered for a long time about this and then the memory faded due to lack of attention.

It was around this time that an event took place that truly changed the course of my life, but at the time I didn't know it. One night a group of what I eventually came to recognize as spirits came to me as I lay awake in my bed. They were dressed in a shimmering gold and silver light and there must have been about five or six of them. I cannot remember if actual words were spoken, but I do remember that this is the time when I was formally introduced to my spirit guide Roger (whose name I learned only much later). I was told that he would be the one taking care of me and my development. I was warned not to speak to anyone about him or what he told me and that there would be consequences if I did. It was not a threat from these benevolent beings, but rather a warning about how the world would deal with a child who saw and spoke to spirits. Someday, the information could be shared, but not now, not until I was grown up.

During this ceremony, I recall that many ideas and concepts were given to me (some of which I will share in this book), but I specifically remember that Roger wanted to prepare me for the future and imparted words to the effect that: "I want to let you know that everything will be all right. There will be much to learn and also much to forget. It will not be an easy path for you, but as long as you keep a pure and loving heart, and try to listen carefully, it will all turn out just fine. Don't worry if you can't understand everything as it happens and also if you forget things along the way. Everything will come out okay in the end. Okay?"

I was confused and suddenly a little scared, but I nodded and managed a little smile as though somewhere in my heart I knew the truth of his words. I could not find the correct path within myself to reach the inside place where I could fully understand what was being said to me. Years later, I was able to connect the old man in the sandbox and the spirit guide to whom I was introduced that night, and knew that both were one and the same, my beloved spirit friend and guide, Roger.

I held the memory of that night's experience for a time and then the incident faded until I could no longer consciously remember Roger, but he had not left; he was always with me and I realize now that I was being trained and given knowledge on an almost subliminal level. Suddenly I would ascertain absolute truths that I had not given any conscious thought to. For example, there was the Scrambled Eggs Theory of Spirituality. This is a name I made up because I needed to call it something to file in my head. I know it was Roger who used this analogy to explain an important concept I needed to become familiar with.

The explanation Roger imparted to me was made as simple as possible, since at that young age, more advanced concepts would have been hard for me to follow. Apparently, because one of my favorite foods back then was (and still is) scrambled eggs, that is the symbol Roger used to explain the Theory of Spirituality.

In some mythologies, it is believed that the universe sprung from an egg. Roger explained to me that the spiritual universe was like scrambled eggs, runny scrambled eggs to be exact. Think of eggs all cracked open and whisked together in a bowl. They are still individual eggs but, at the same time, they are being mixed together to become one big "eggness." As these cook, they form into one mass, but because these are runny eggs, some of these, though still attached, stream away from the mass of eggs. When a child is born, that little runny part enters him or her and is his or her soul or spirit. The runny part is still attached to the larger aggregate, but it is also in the person, so the person is separate yet also always attached to the main mass of eggs. Then when the person dies, the runny part of the egg, the soul or spirit, returns to the egg mass to become one again with the cosmic whole of which it was a part all along although it appeared to be separate.

All of this made perfect sense to me then, and is the story I sometimes tell people to help them understand how it is that we are all connected and how I am able to do what I do. I also remember that for a while I was reluctant to eat scrambled eggs because I was afraid of eating someone else's soul.

My parents did not know anything about my perceptions of reality. They did not realize my amazing joy in the blossoming of a flower or the agony I felt when I was near another in pain or saw an event on TV that was horrific enough in itself, but for me was doubly painful because of my ability to not only identify with the person in pain, but to physically feel the distress or the sorrow or the wounds of another.

When I was seven years old, I was home from school with a cold, lying in bed, dozing, when I suddenly was overcome with an overwhelming sense of fear and sorrow. I looked around my room to see if anything might be causing this feeling and for a moment thought that perhaps it was something I was visiting in a dream or in that half-conscious state of almost dream. As I came to full consciousness, I realized that the feelings were growing in intensity. Suddenly, I felt an overwhelming urge to turn on the TV. Normally, I wasn't allowed to watch television during the day, so I tiptoed quietly down the hallway and into the living room, past the kitchen where my mother was preparing my lunch of chicken soup with rice. Anxiously hesitant, I reached for the ON button on the TV. As the black-and-white picture expanded onto the screen, I could see a visibly shaken Walter Cronkite remove his glasses, saying that President Kennedy had died at 12:25 p.m. of a gunshot.

My mother, hearing the TV come on, came quickly into the room to reprimand me for turning on the TV in the middle of the day. She opened her mouth to speak, but she too, was stunned to see the image of the usually staid Cronkite having a deeply emotional reaction to something.

"What's going on?" she asked me, ready to scold me for being out of bed.

"Someone killed the President," I replied in a soft, shocked voice.

"Oh, no," my mother sank into the chair closest to the TV, her hand covering her mouth. I went over to her and gave her a hug to make her feel better, my own agony still pulsing in me.

It was odd, though, that I was able to feel the sorrow of an event so removed from my immediate environment, but I could not sense my mother's sadness more than to acknowledge that she was sad. It was not a feeling that entered my being to thus become part of my personal experience. I would always wonder about this—my openness to the joys and sorrows of others, but not to those closest to me. It was almost as though there was a wall that separated me from my parents, especially my mother. I could sense my own feelings, but not hers. I could feel something happening hundreds of miles away, but the tears of my mother were something I could see and feel bad about, but not sense from her perspective.

My mother was oblivious to this as we sat watching the events unfold before us in Dallas. She did not even ask me why I was out of bed or what had made me turn on the TV at that moment. It was one of the few times that I had exhibited an external reaction to my perception of an occurrence. Normally, especially in the future as my ability to feel the emotions of another intensified, I was able to contain my reactions. I believed it was better to enter almost a daydream state and appear absentminded than to have to explain what was happening inside of me at that moment. So, my parents came to believe that I was a dreamer and that I sometimes was unable to pay attention or concentrate on a matter at hand when, quite to the contrary, I was so focused on the meat of the moment that I was unable or unwilling to communicate.

"Pay attention, Tobie," they would say, my teachers would say, the crossing guard would say, but I was paying attention, more closely than they could know.

Not that I was in a constantly heightened state of awareness. Oftentimes, days would pass when I was able to live a relatively normal life. I would play games in the park with my friends, watch TV, learn in school, and not one thing would trigger my clairvoyant ability. Then, unexpectedly, without warning, I would encounter someone who would seemingly need to share, unknowingly, his or her pain, or sometimes, if I was lucky, happiness. For reasons I never understood, I was more likely to feel another individual's pains or concerns than their joys. I knew the intense sensation of elation when the space around me became so clear and crystalline and defined that it seemed that someone had washed the air molecules and set them to sparkling around me. It seemed, though, that other people broadcast their pains more readily than their joys. I sometimes wondered if they felt pleasure or that maybe my lack of perceiving it in them was because they didn't experience it in themselves. Many people, it seemed, were more frequently in a semi-suffering state than a state of pure happiness. As I grew older I realized that this must be true and I came to see that alcohol and drugs were often used by people to try to cover their pain. I, however, knew the truth. It seemed the more someone drank or did drugs around me, the more deeply searing their pain became.

My parents, oblivious to my internalization of the next four days in November, let me stay up day and night watching the events unfold in Dallas and Washington. Distressed as they were, they never realized that I was sitting there sensing the sorrow of Mrs. Kennedy and her children, and the shock and pain in the hearts of the many people interviewed all over the country that weekend. I felt inside of myself a call to witness the events unfolding before me in black-and-white on the TV, but exploding in full color within my heart and soul.

For weeks afterward, as the country began the long journey to healing, I carried the heavy sadness in my heart and for me one question remained—how did I know to get out of bed and turn on the TV at that moment? What force or idea or being had communicated to me the need for the action on my part? And why weren't my parents aware of the strangeness of my actions? The wall between me and them seemed impenetrable. I could not sense them, could not feel them in my heart. Although I loved them both dearly and knew they loved me, the love seemed to float around them as a concept, lacking a concreteness my encounters with others seemed to display.

Not all my empathic perceptions were on a massive scale. Sometimes it was the simple, mundane moments that would throw me for a loop, especially as I grew older. I remember one incident in high school that stands out, even though it was a comparatively small one.

I hadn't seen my friend Martha in our English class and decided she must have gotten sick and left school. I entered the vocal music room for chorus, my last class of the day. I loved to sing and enjoyed the camaraderie of learning and polishing the songs we sung in class. I didn't particularly care for performing—too many eyes on me. My adrenaline would make me more nervous and sometimes dizzy, and fear would make each step onto the risers feel as though I were lifting blocks of cement instead of my feet. Singing with my classmates didn't bother me too much, as though the act of expressing myself creatively overrode my usual discomfort. It seemed the music blocked that portion of my brain that otherwise was spinning around thoughts I was unable to control.

I took my place in the second soprano section, picking up the music folder on my chair. Before I could remove the first song, Martha came in and sat down beside me. We nodded at each other as the choir director took his place before the group and signaled the pianist to play the scales for warm up. As each section followed the notes up and down the keyboard, I started to feel a strange sensation in my mouth, a dull ache that seemed to be growing in my gums and reaching into each tooth. I could feel a throbbing in my sinuses as the pain increased and my eyes moistened in reaction. I raised my hand and excused myself from the room.

Leaning against the wall in the hallway, I realized that my discomfort was slowly ebbing and I took a few breaths to compose myself. I thought of going to the nurse's office, but my rapid recovery erased the reason to go. I couldn't understand what was happening, but as I looked at my watch, I realized that fifteen minutes remained to the class and I decided to go back in.

As soon as I sat down, the sensations began again, but not quite as intensely as the first time, as though I had somehow become inured in some small measure to the pain. I sang as best I could and then, finally, class was over. I turned to Martha to say something about how weird the pain was when Martha turned to me and said that that had been a hard class to sit through since her mouth hurt so badly from having had her braces tightened. It was kind of weird, though, she said, because the pain seemed to ease up for a bit just before I had left the room and again when I had returned.

I blinked quickly as I realized that that was the pain I had felt . . . Martha's pain had become my own and apparently, somehow, my experience of the pain had eased Martha's discomfort. I had no idea how to absorb this information. I needed time to think this one through. Once outside, on the way home, I walked slowly, trying to sort this newest experience into the strange filing cabinet of my life.

My grandparents had an old beach house in Winthrop, Massachusetts. Each summer, my family would go there for a week and the cousins from nearby Brookline would come out and play with us on the beach that curved like a giant arm cradling the ocean. A latticework archway supporting vining roses led to the house, which was wrapped by a porch from front door to side door. There was always at least one child in diapers and so there was always an odor of soiled diaper, baby powder, and sea air. The grass in the small yard was rough and scraggly and walking barefoot was a challenge. It was a short walk to the beach and usually a group of cousins went out mid-morning with beach satchels, shovels and pails, towels, beach chairs, diaper bags, and an available adult to explore the beach and enjoy the sun.

I was the oldest of the cousins and although I enjoyed their company, as I grew older, I needed quiet moments of my own. I remember being on the beach alone early one day, enjoying the solitude and lost in the thoughts only a 13-year old girl would entertain, because, through everything else that was going on, part of me remained a "normal" child.

In the intimate vastness of the moment, I felt a stillness and heard a profound silence not even the rhythmic waves nor my own breathing nor my heartbeat could diminish. I felt the calmness envelope my heart and reach deeply into my soul. Slowly, I became aware of another sound so sweet that I could feel my taste buds quiver. It was a sound that seemed to float on an aroma of rose buds and lilacs. It was a sound like none other I had ever heard. I strained to hear each note, each increment of harmony as it washed over me in wave upon wave of magnificent music so intensely sweet that I did not need to question its origin—the universe seemed to be singing to me, not one voice or instrument, but a multitude of nameless nuances of sound, each melding and blending with the next. I felt the spinning of each planet, each star, and the sweeping of the galaxies were all producing the music for me.

My bare feet clung to the moist sand beneath them, my arms stretched out to gather in the symphony seeking to soothe my soul. My heart filled with joy and, despite the empty beach around me, I sensed a multitude of loving beings. I could not name what I was sensing, but suddenly I felt my place in the oneness around me and in me. Suddenly I felt a sound within me that wished to be expressed, that wanted to break free of me. It felt like a tingling hum that started in my toes and spread throughout my body until my mouth opened and I sang out a vibrant perfect note back into the universe. I held the note as long as I could and then seemingly beyond what breath I had. As my note ceased, so too did the music around me.

I slowly became aware of my surroundings and was glad no one had been around to hear my impromptu response to the cosmos. I blushed slightly at the thought that somehow, someone had seen or heard me, although I was quite sure I was alone. I did not know what to call what I had experienced, did not know where it had come from. Since then, I have learned about the idea of planetary music, though still I wondered if it was something real that had occurred or if it was just some symbol that had been made tangible for me. I like to believe that, in fact, the planets do sing, the universe had indeed sung to me, and somehow my body knew, or maybe recalled, how to respond, to join the chorus. I sat down on the sand and reflected on what this had taught me since, even at this tender age, I realized that a lot was being given to me although I did not know how or why. Even as the experience began to fade from my immediate awareness of it, I began to question its reality. Had it really happened? Was I losing my mind? The small voice inside me reassured me that, no, this had not been a figment of my imagination. My sense of oneness was not ebbing, the joy in my heart was still swelling, and the music seemed to still be echoing in my soul.

The strangest thing for me, especially as I grew older, was the realization that I could not sense any emotion from my parents, especially my mother. They appeared to be shut down from me, although they seemed to relate to each other. I knew I could feel the deepest sorrow of a stranger, but not the merest emotion behind my mother's smile. I wondered, as time went on, if it had something to do with shared biology or genetic codes. Were they so similar physically that I could not sense their emotions? I called the feeling "the wall." I never really understood if the wall boxed them away from me or me away from them. Either way, I knew, from a very young age, that my parents would not be able to understand my ability to perceive the pain or, more rarely, the joy of another. They did not seem to see the world the same way in which I did, did not see the vibrancy of colors or sounds, did not experience the "lightening and brightening." They did not feel the pain of a neighbor's fall, although they did make sympathetic sounds after they heard of the incident much later, as the neighbor came hobbling home from the hospital, ankle in a cast and leaning on crutches.

When I was very little, sometimes I would have a brief intense moment of clarity, see a flower vibrate with bright color, the hues wafting above the flower like a fragrant heat moiré. I would then rush inside to tell my mother and she would look at me strangely and say how nice that was while under her breath she would comment on my vivid imagination.

The trouble was that usually when I was sensing something—pain, joy, sorrow—I would become frozen in place as though my body had ceased to have any import and it was the space inside of me that was the only living part of me. I would freeze in place, stopped, mesmerized into inaction. On those unfortunate occasions when this would happen when my mother or teacher was around, they would invariably call me up short, telling me to pay attention and to stop daydreaming. Thoroughly immersed in whatever I was experiencing, I would be unable to respond or react and my mother would repeat herself until through no will of hers, the sensations would subside, as though I had drunk the last drop of the experience and I would blink and move back into the reality I shared with other people.

In my late teens, circumstances arose that partially outed me from the paranormal closet, so-to-speak. I became involved in paranormal investigations and other activities that brought my interest in and involvement with spirit out into the open. I will discuss these in detail later on, but suffice it to say that at that time, I believed my mother attributed my emotional state to some teenage angst problem, or that I was on drugs or perhaps becoming psychotic or schizophrenic. Apparently, she decided I needed to speak with a professional and so she made an appointment to see a psychiatrist.

I did not know what to say to this man. In fact I only vaguely remember saying anything, though I am quite sure I answered honestly that I saw ghosts and talked to spirits. The doctor prescribed a little blue triangular pill. I was not happy on the pill, nor was I sad. In fact, I felt nothing whatsoever, as though I was walking around in a daze. I stopped taking the pills after three weeks, although I didn't tell my mother right away.

Recently I found out that the real reason my mother had taken me to the psychiatrist was indeed because I said I saw ghosts and spirits. I had broken Roger's number one rule not to tell them what I could do. But I was nineteen by then and had experienced enough in the paranormal world to know that certain events were real and verifiable. At the time, I was living in Fredonia, NY, and experiencing some very serious paranormal incidents.

As I mulled the new information over, that my mother had indeed taken me to a doctor because I saw those in the spirit plane, I could only think of one question that remained to ask her. Did anyone bother to find out if the ghosts and spirits did, indeed, exist?

Chapter 2

The Gift of Knowledge:
Who and What are Spirits, Ghosts, and Entities

I Sing the Body Electric.
(Walt Whitman)
There is no death, there are no dead.
(National Spiritualist Association of Churches)

What are these things that go bump in the night? Is it the cat simply jumping down from the forbidden countertop? Or is it something more? Something less tangible? Why do we become more cognizant of that something else at night rather than during the daylight hours? Well, that one is easy . . . we are more relaxed, the TV is turned off, we are quieting our minds and allowing the distractions of the day to fall away. The phone isn't ringing, dinner has been made and cleaned up after, all is calm and peaceful. Now is the time our minds are most receptive to visitors from the other here. While they are always around us, trying to capture our attention if so need be, we are able to hear their faint call when our minds are more receptive, in the still quiet hours of the night.

This is not to say that visitations do not take place 24/7. These do. Many of the examples of communication that I will discuss later in this chapter did, indeed, occur during the day in all manner of circumstances. But most séances and paranormal investigations occur at night, when we are more receptive, not necessarily when it is more convenient for them to contact us!

What differentiates a ghost from an entity from a spirit? Some would say there is little difference, but it has been my experience that there are different levels of communication, manifestation, and interaction in these energy levels. A ghost is an apparition; it is a portion of the spirit being that becomes stuck in a time and place due to the sudden loss of the body or an unfounded belief that that location is where they are supposed to stay, waiting for something to happen to take them somewhere else.

Ghosts are entities who once were incarnate and, rather than moving to the next plane upon physical transition, become trapped in a time and place of importance to them either because of strong emotion (love, hate, fear), or a connection to a moment or individual in the place (a marriage or a violent death of a loved one). A ghost is an imprint of characteristics of the person who has actually passed. The spirit of the person becomes mired in a holding pattern and is unable to make the full transition. The spirit exists and so does its ghost as a projection. That projection is often dressed in period appropriate clothing at the time of physical death, although the spirit itself is timeless.

Oftentimes, there is a repetitiveness of motion or behavior or sounds that takes place associated with the person's life and/or moments of death. While sometimes ghosts can interact benevolently with their surroundings (a ghost in Yonkers, New York, left jewelry for the occupants of the house), often they are oblivious to those around them and the passage of time (ghosts of castles, e.g.). Since benevolent or lost ghosts are trapped in space and time, it is best to get them to move on to the other side so they can reintegrate with their spirit self, rest, and prepare for their next incarnation.

While hauntings can be interesting and sometimes entertaining, it is always best for the ghost's spirit to move on. In Fredonia, New York, where I attended college for a short time and lived for slightly longer, a group interested in the paranormal conducted several investigations to connect with six young women who attended the State Normal School, a precursor to the State University of New York system, and a janitor who died in a fire in the Normal School building, which also housed the dormitory. The fire occurred on December 14, 1900, and since then, strange noises and movements had been witnessed from passersby to the rebuilt and subsequently abandoned building (at the time of our investigation).

Our band of amateur paranormal investigators visited the building (nicknamed "Old Main") twice on our own and the third time accompanied by Ed and Loraine Warren, who researched the "Amityville Horror" house, and members of their investigative team. Several ghosts were encountered, and because the building had been rebuilt, they often seemed to be gliding above the floors, though actually, they were still walking on the original floors of the building, which were several inches higher than those of the rebuilt one. One member of the team encountered a man in a red and black plaid flannel shirt in the boiler room in the basement. Our teammate described the man as having thick hair, heavy jowls, and an Irish brogue. He appeared to be intoxicated, and was heard half singing "I see you are here."

Several other ghosts were spotted and heard throughout the various nights spent in the building, including a girl in an illuminated dress in the auditorium. We could also hear a choir of girls singing, accompanied by an organ.

After our investigation was completed, we conducted research at the town's archives and discovered pictures of the girls and the janitor, all of whom were recognizable as the ghosts we had seen during our investigations.

At the end of our research, we gathered together to send the ghosts of the girls and the janitor love and release. While I cannot verify the success of this, I can testify that townspeople ceased to perceive the sounds and sights of a haunted Old Main.

Another entity that was witnessed in the building during our research was a dark shadowy, apparently male figure in the balcony of the auditorium blocking half the window behind him. The two of us who had witnessed this turned towards each other to discuss this occurrence. When we turned back, the light from outside was pouring through the entire unblocked window, the figure having disappeared. In photos taken during the investigation, this same sort of figure was seen sitting in the auditorium.

Being less experienced than I am now with such things, I somehow permitted the entity to follow me home. Lying in bed, I could hear a rustling in the papers on my desk and looked up to see the entity standing there. Thankfully, Roger, my guide, helped me to extricate this being from my apartment. It is as simple as asking the being to leave. I have always tried to keep these sorts of beings outside of my environment, but when any happen by, I simply command them to go away. Methods other than or in addition to a simple request include sprinkling salt (sea salt is best) on the thresholds and windowsills of the living quarters. If the entity is particularly "sticky" (i.e., does not seem to want to leave), employing the symbols of the cross can help alleviate this lower vibration infestation. Perhaps because of the long association of the cross in fighting such entities, most of these lower beings have a negative reaction to this symbol and leave quite readily.

Entities come in many forms. Both spirits and elementals are considered entities and different ones exist on different planes, which can be of a higher or lower nature. It's all energy, as are we, and this energy can take on many different forms and intelligence levels.

Elementals are a form of entity known as nature spirits—these are beings that are not and have never incarnated in human form, but nonetheless enjoy an existence on other planes. Some take the forms of humans or animals and some interact and tend to the natural realms, like the devas who help with vegetable propagation in Findhorn, an eco-spiritual community in Scotland. The devas work to ensure a healthy and bountiful crop. They also seem to help create incredibly large vegetable specimens.

Elementals can be benevolent or malevolent. The former seek to help incarnate beings while the latter enjoy inflicting discomfort and even harm on humans. The movie *The Exorcist* is about a malevolent elemental that was brought into the home through the unwise use of a Ouija board. Using this sort of communication instrument without proper training and protection can result in negative energies coming through to communicate and overstaying their welcome long after the board has been put away. What one thinks might be a deceased boyfriend is actually a malevolent energy feeding off information and energy from within the incarnate participants. Left to their own devices, these elementals can wreak havoc in a person's life. Poltergeists are negative elementals that also utilize the hyper energies of those in puberty or with diminished mental capacity. Oftentimes, it can be difficult to rid oneself of these beings.

On the other hand, there are spiritual teachers and guides, some of whom have been incarnate, like my guide, Roger, and some of whom have spent their entire existence on other planes. Spirit guides choose to work with us from the other dimensions that co-exist with ours (more on this later) in order to make sure we have help when we need it. They are with us from birth, though I don't remember Roger any earlier than when I was about four years old. For the most part, I find that Roger stays pretty much in the background, and I have to suspect he has a life on the other side that does not necessary have anything to do with me. There are many times, however, that I know he is near and wishing to be helpful and so I listen carefully to discern any information he wishes to impart. Right now, for example, he is indicating that sometimes it is difficult to get my attention and at those times he needs to give me a jolt through synchronistic moments (which I will also discuss later) or strange occurrences calculated to make sure I turn to him for guidance.

Over time, I have remembered a previous incarnate life in Dover, England, in the mid-1800s when Roger and I were friends. We had been involved with paranormal inquiry, which was becoming popular during our previous incarnation together. Knowing that I would be pursuing the paranormal and helping to guide people to a realization of spirit in my current physical manifestation, he decided to stay in spirit to help from that side.

Teachers who primarily live on higher planes are called by all sorts of titles, including Masters. They seem to have knowledge of many different planes and levels of existence and for the most part serve to inspire those who are receptive to their vibrations. Sometimes, these masters incarnate in hopes of inspiring the masses. Their incarnate lives and teachings exist to move the earth plane along in its development. Unfortunately, this practice often results in deep confusion and ultimately distorts their words and has proven, for the most part, ineffective in the long run. Most advanced teachers remain discarnate and inspire from the other realms.

And then, there is spirit, which includes our fundamental selves, whether incarnate or discarnate.

In Japan there is a greeting, Namaste, which means the spirit in me bows to the spirit in you. Another subtle interpretation of this salutation is my spirit bows to your spirit. There is an understanding that our essential selves are not physical, but rather spiritual.

Before we are born into a physical body, we live in another dimension co-existing with this one. This is but one of many simultaneous co-spatial and cohabitating dimensions and planes of existence. These times and spaces live in the same apparent time/space that we do and while ours, for the most part, seems to have limited awareness of the others, entities on these other planes are well aware of us. When we are preparing to incarnate, we take stock of our level of progression and analyze what it is we need to learn and experience for our spiritual growth to continue. Sometimes this growth occurs through hardship, and sometimes through a life of ease.

When we incarnate into our bodies at approximately the time of birth, we can come and go easily. We are not tied in, so to speak. After a short while, with the overwhelming input from the physical senses, we acclimate to our physical boundaries, and with the acquisition of language, our transition into the physical world is complete. Language seems to force upon us a manner of communication that seems to preclude non-verbal communication, i.e., telepathy, etc. While it is possible to work on this means of communication, and some are able to continue using this method, most find themselves mired in the concreteness of language. The word apple means a physical apple, but does not, in everyday understanding, indicate the essence of that apple.

When a spirit loses that sense of real self, this world appears to be all there is. On the one hand, remembering would certainly improve how we treat each other and our selves. But on the other hand, it would seem that some lessons on this plane are best learned when this plane is all one concerns oneself with. Our real selves, our spirits, become a target of fear and distrust (how do we trust what we cannot see?) and this probably explains why horror films and films about the supernatural are so popular. We are using these to experience, in the only way we know how, our true selves whose existence we are denying.

There are some who remain on the cusp between this world and the non-physical one (which has a "solidity" to it when we are on that side . . . i.e., it is not all filmy white wispiness). Many people who hear voices, who refrain or seem to be prohibited from fully interacting with this physical plane, are actually living with one spiritual foot here, and one spiritual foot "there."

We live our lives and become enamored of our existence here, having forgotten that other place in which we also live. Then we fear leaving here, not knowing that there is another place to go to, a place from which we came, and a place that our true selves, our real essence, call home.

While leaving the body can sometimes be painful or traumatic, finding ourselves on the other side can be a relief from long illness, for example.

Barb's Aunt Liddy was raised a devout Catholic in the days before Vatican II. Even after she went to live with my cousin Lou and his wife Barb, her niece, she maintained traditional Catholic beliefs. She knew that when she died, if she followed the tenets set down by the Church, she would go to heaven. Barb's Aunt Liddy died (or, more appropriately, transitioned, i.e., shifted her spirit from the physical plane to the next plane of existence) Memorial Day Weekend, May 30, 2004, five weeks before my dad transitioned on July 5. Liddy's death came as a shock to Barb and to Liddy herself, who had given no indication that she might be preparing for transitioning. I will let Barb share her perspective of the days following Liddy's transitioning:

> 6/1/04: This was the night before her funeral. I went to bed that night saying to myself that I needed help getting through the funeral—in light of my being so close to her, and her dying so suddenly—and to help my son, Marc, through the day. I kept saying, "you have to help me though this—help me." I had brought to the funeral home two dresses, and I had told the mortician to bury her in the appropriate one. Both were black—one knit, and the other one a coat dress. I really thought he would choose the coatdress; I thought it was dressier. I also had mentioned to him not to set her hair—Liddy had naturally curly hair—just let it dry naturally and

to use natural pink make-up—I did not want her to look "made up."

That night I dreamt of walking into the funeral home, and walking into the first room on the left. Liddy was in the black knit dress, her hair and make-up were just as I wanted these to be. There were three arrangements of roses to her left and three to the right.

On the day of the funeral, the funeral director was waiting for us outside. I asked where to go and he said to go to the first room on the left. I walked in and Liddy was wearing the black knit dress, her hair and make-up were just as I had seen these the night before, and there were six arrangements of roses—three to the left and three to the right. It was exactly as I had seen it in my "dream." Marc was extremely upset, but I was able to help him because I had already "been there" the night before.

6/2/04: My husband Louis had always told me that he believes that when a person dies, "the lights go out—that's it." Louis said he had a dream about Liddy coming to answer the door to let him in. He said she looked so young, and she answered the door so full of energy. She said, "let me show you my NEW home, I love it so much; I am so happy." She ran upstairs, almost running up two steps at a time.

Not long after Liddy died, I had a dream of walking into a church—Liddy was in a pew saying to me "I'm saving you a place."

9/15/04: I asked my mother about Liddy and why she had moved out of her Yates Street house in Albany, and how she had moved the furniture all by herself, and what date had she moved on. My mother said she did not know, but would ask her sister, Pat. I felt all along I had asked Liddy every question I had had, so only this last question remained. This last question kept bothering me, and I wanted to know the answer. In the meantime, I had been hoping that I had kept Liddy's letters to me, but I was afraid I had not. Liddy wrote me many letters over the years. I looked in a bag of stuff Monday and found nothing. I took the bag out again on Tuesday, and I found the letters! I found the exact date and year I needed—1977—and all the answers to all my remaining questions. In the letters, Liddy mentioned the roof leaking in her house and being afraid of the rain, because of water damage to her house. She mentioned getting rid of the furniture, having only chairs and tables left. She dated the letter 1977—and now I knew the date! She mentioned "loving her new home" (in the same way she had in Louis's dream). All this was very important to me because in later letters, Liddy mostly asked questions she wanted me to answer. In these letters, she did not ask me questions—she gave me the information I needed.

1/28/05: I had a dream that Louis and I were on a driving trip. We had just left a vacation house, and Louis was driving. I get carsick so I usually drive; that Louis was driving in my dream was quite unusual. While passing a house, I saw Liddy stooping down on the porch. As our car passed, she looked at me in an unusual 3-D piercing manner, so that her face seemed to be traveling directly to my face. I told Louis to stop the car. I ran to the porch, and asked some children there where my Aunt Liddy had gone. They pointed up. I ran upstairs to an almost closed bedroom door. The door was open only a crack, through which I saw only a blue bathrobe. I talked with Liddy through the door telling her I was there in the house before. She said she knew I was there. We both had to use the bathroom then; there were two bathrooms side by side. We were both in there a long time talking through the wall. I was telling Liddy about the trip, telling her I loved her, and then I told her I had to leave, but that we'd be together again soon. While upstairs, talking with her, I never saw her face. In the dream, she was not hard of hearing, as she had been in life. This dream was especially important to me because I did not have a chance to say good-bye to Liddy. She had died suddenly in the hospital; I was outside her door when she passed away.

I believe it is interesting to note that while Barb was interested in the paranormal and in my involvement with that realm, she really did not have confidence or understanding in what was happening in the time after Liddy's transition. I marveled with her when the letters seemingly appeared out of nowhere and then explained the idea of there being a veil between the physical and spirit dimensions, similar to the separation in the last entry above. A wall between the two of them made perfect sense to me, and the knowledge about the veil seemed to give Barb additional comfort.

Over four years after Liddy's transition, Barb and I were talking and she mentioned to me that she had recently searched in the box again to see if there were any more letters or documents. She then realized that the only letters she ever found were the five or six that directly answered her questions about Liddy's house and move!

My dad transitioned about five weeks after Barb's aunt. He had suffered for many years from COPD, specifically emphysema brought on by years of smoking. He was hospitalized early in June 2004. He believed that when your life on earth was finished, that was it, nothing existed on the other end of birth but the black hole of death. I always told him that he might indeed be mistaken and when he got over to the other side, and found that he still existed, he should give me a sign to let me know that I was right and he was wrong. He would shake his head and sigh at my delusional thinking.

During his four-week stay at the hospital and one week stay at hospice, dad had some interesting experiences. A scientist in life (a geologist specializing in paleontology, along with environmental science), dad's observational skills were not lost in this exploration.

At one point he said, "I don't know how to get where I'm supposed to go," and "I was dead this morning and then I woke up." His roommate was a man in the final stages of cancer who moaned and screamed continually while my dad and he shared a room. Dad saw a large group of his roommate's relatives visit in the middle of the night. They were dressed in their Sunday best and came en masse to visit their loved one. My dad never could wrap his mind around the fact that the man had not had a visitation of a physical nature in the middle of the night and that what he had seen were relatives who had already passed on preparing the man to do so also.

At another point, dad was waking up and said to "get that person out of here," to "make that person leave." We asked if he knew who it was and he said no. Since there wasn't any physical person there, I felt strongly that he was perceiving a helping spirit from the other side, one who is sent to help the transition process.

On July 4, 2004, it was quite evident that my dad, who had been administered morphine to calm him down during the process, was in his last hours incarnate. I kept thinking that it would be quite fitting if he passed on the Fourth of July, since he had always been very patriotic and had served as a ball turret gunner in World War II. I needed to leave to get my children from my mother's house, and I sensed that this was spirit's ploy to get me to leave so that dad could also leave. Sometimes, people in the transition process will hang on until they are alone or with minimal company in order to leave. I gave him a hug and softly sang "Me and My Shadow" to him, a song we had always sung as we climbed the stairs to his mother's apartment in Rockland, Massachusetts, and told him it was okay to go and be with grandma.

At 2:45 a.m., a call from the hospice informed me that my dad had transitioned at 1:43 a.m. Immediately, I felt compelled to take his WWII photo and look at the back of it, slipping it out of its leather frame to do so. Earlier in the day, at the hospice, my daughter Jane had read from 1 Corinthians 13 about the greatest of these is love. On the back of the picture, inscribed to my mother, he had written, "The greatest thing - - - Phil." I knew immediately this was a sign from him. Despite making copies of the photo over the years, I do not recall ever seeing those words there, and if I had seen them, had forgotten they were there. Here was the first of many signs that dad gave me over the next year, including yellow roses (the flowers he had given me on the day of my birth) that bloomed on a rose bush I didn't even know was in my garden. The roses bloomed on specific days, such as his funeral several days later, and on his sister's birthday late in September.

For one full year, my dad continued to give me signs that he was indeed alive. After a year, communication with him became more sporadic, like phone calls from a very busy spirit. Life does not end at transition, and spirit needs to stay close to loved ones in the time following this. In addition to Barb's and my own experiences, I have spoken to others who also noticed that communication from loved ones on the other side seems to become less frequent after the first year. I believe that the discarnate relative realizes that the incarnate loved one is acclimating to life in the physical plane without them. On the other hand, spirit continues to have a life on the other side, with experiences and responsibilities.

We have such a limited range of perceptions here. We cannot even fathom how people from different cultures, religions, and environments live in far off countries (or even in nearby enclaves, for example ultra orthodox religious groups and their modes of conduct and mores). It would astonish most of us that people really do move about on camels or rickshaws, or do not eat certain foods or not eat for long periods of time. Our current world tensions are caused in part by our inability to grasp the idea that not everybody is like us or even should be like us. Then how much harder is it to comprehend that there are other levels of existence, some co-existing in the same space as we are, that we cannot see or hear or sense?

People in the other dimensions, which I sometimes refer to as the other here, have lives just like we do. Their lives appear physical and material to them in another vibrational level. My table is solid because I am solid; their table is solid on their plane in their experience of what constitutes physical.

It doesn't matter what you believe; it matters what the truth is. Our belief systems give us comfort while we are incarnate and shape our transitioning experience. Many of the world's religions address what is expected of the individual in order to attain the desired outcome in so-called death. If you follow all the rules and do what is required of you, you will go to heaven and continue to experience a blessed existence. And indeed, when people of certain religious leanings pass on, they are met by the religious figures they expect to meet. In near death experiences, some of those who return speak of seeing Jesus in the light at the end of the tunnel. Of course, those who expect to see other figures, do see them, always within the light. In actuality, the light is there, since we here on earth are essentially living in the darkness of ignorance and fear, and the light one sees upon transitioning is merely the opening of one's eyes to the truth of one's nature. Certain religions even require specific rites associated with passing over and even how burials are to be conducted. And if one's experience is that which has been shaped by religion, then eventually helpers appear to show the truth of the new existence.

It is interesting to note that not one person I have talked to on the other side has ever mentioned religion or any religious figures. Even when I can ascertain from the sitter that the person would have been devoutly religious, when they communicate from the other here, they do not seem to have any need to express a religious context to their current existence.

How is it possible to communicate with spiritual beings, including the discarnate and never incarnate? I believe it can be explained by examining the limitations of our perceptions on this plane, and what that plane really means. We are bound by three dimensions. We can think of these in terms of the period or dot representing the first dimension, the line representing the second dimension, and a cube representing the third dimension. If you try to think past the idea of the cube (or orb, or pyramid, or us), you most likely will be met with a brick wall, which appears 2D, but is really 3D. Your perception of the brick wall is different from the reality of the brick wall.

In addition, there is a 4th dimension, which we perceive as time. We perceive this thing called time as fluid, but moving in only one direction, forward. When you think of now, by the time you have thought "now" that moment is already in the past. Now, in reality, is infinitesimally small, less than a thought. As we project a moment into the future, it slides through now into the past. We can remember the past, but we cannot relive it in our limited perception of time (although we must remember that George Santayana said, "those who cannot remember the past are condemned to repeat it," but I assume this means the things we need to learn from, and not a delightful Sunday afternoon in our youth).

Being able to measure something, to quantify it, gives it a quality of recognizability and a validity in existence as we understand it, limited as we are to four dimensions, three spatial and one temporal.

In *Flatland*, a brilliant book by mathematician Edwin Abbott, and told by the main character, A. Square, Lineland consists of points. This would be a 1-dimensional world. Flatland consists of flat figures, such as A. Square, the narrator, and circles, and triangles. This would be a 2-dimensional world. Spaceland consists of solids, like cubes, orbs, and pyramids. This would be a 3-dimensional world. Each of these dimensions lacks the understanding to perceive and comprehend the next dimension in any but the most abstract terms. A point living on a line has not the experiential knowledge that a square has, for example, and thus cannot knowingly admit the square's existence.

These dimensions are "this plane" paradigms—and may in reality be illusory. The concept that other dimensions would also adhere to these dimensional precepts may in itself be a fallacy. In the greater reality, this separation of dimensions and this apparent order or hierarchy of dimensions may be an illusion, or at least a false reality. How do we know what is real versus what has been so reinforced in our own communal awareness that we have created our perceptions of this reality, rather than perceiving some actual reality independent of our sensory perception? And, since for the most part, we are perceiving this reality through the limitations of our five senses, which differ to some degree from one person to the next, how accurate can this perceiving be?

But what if we could expand our perceptions and discern the next spatial dimension, or the one after that, or the one after that? And what if these weren't separate dimensions at all, but different expressions of here and now, all existing at the same time, and yet separated by our perceptions and understanding and not by an actual separateness? What then if all times were now and all spaces were here?

If all of this were accessible, we would be aware that Great Aunt Lucy didn't actually die, but merely stepped out of her physical body into another room. We would be able to visit and talk to her any time we liked and everyone would be able to communicate freely with the dearly not-so-departed.

Instead, now, many people who wish to speak to loved ones who have transitioned, and get responses from them, must employ the services of a medium, one who is aware of that "other" dimension and is able to establish communication with those living there.

Do those who live with the knowledge of spirit ever doubt? Yes, but then at just the right moment, proof sifts through the veil to shake us back to reality and reaffirm the spiritual levels of existence, both incarnate and discarnate. When I was younger, and got tired of being different, I would try to set aside my ability to perceive more deeply into the spiritual realm. Then something, some event or action would take place that would reaffirm my purpose and the real reality. Often this pulling me up short felt like being gently chastised for doubting, but at other times, it was like a brick to the head. Once, when I doubted that I had actually experienced a knowing, spirit led me to my car and guided my hand on the wheel until, far out into the country, in front of me I saw the exact strange image I had seen in my mind's eye while in trance at home, that of a very large and tall mound of earth with a 90-degree wedge removed from it. Sometimes, working with spirit

is less a walk in the park, than a ride in the country . . .
an interesting, wonder-filled, and ethereal country.

Chapter 3

The Gift of Counsel:
First Readings

There is a world of communication that is not dependent on words.
(Mary Martin)

Our five senses are very limited as far as the range of available vibrations we can perceive. Indeed, it is but a small portion of the light spectrum we can see, and dogs can hear sounds we cannot. In addition, different people perceive the world differently, e.g., no two people see exactly the same tint of blue in exactly the same way. Differences in the cones in the retina and in the material being viewed can alter the perception of color. We can both be looking at a blue ball, for example, and perceive a slight difference in the color's tonality. We would not even be aware of this, unless we discuss our perceptions, and even then our ability to describe what we see and impart that perception is additionally hindered by the words selected on the part of the speaker and the comprehension of those words on the part of the listener.

Then consider the challenge of seeing and hearing spirit and being able to impart that information to a sitter. With practice, it becomes easier, but until I receive confirmation from the sitter of the accuracy of the information, I am left to wonder if anything I am saying is valid.

So, is it my five senses that perceive spirit, or does my incarnate spirit perceive spirit discarnate? Is it my spirit-self and its faculties of perception that are perceiving that other spirit? Then, is this "spirit sensory data" somehow fed through the physical sensory apparatus to allow the perception of spirit image and sound?

I was trained primarily by Roger, though it was more the process of natural development of an ability, like walking or talking, than actual lessons. This mode of learning was augmented by reading, and by observation of other mediums of what to do <u>and</u> what <u>not</u> to do.

Mediums perceive information from a non-physical source, normally discarnate spirit, and relate that information to a person, frequently referred to as a sitter, who is seeking communication with that spirit, oftentimes a loved one. It is gratifying to receive immediate confirmation that the information, often personal and obscure, is relevant to the sitter. Readings are performed on a one-to-one basis and also in circles known as séances. In a séance, or in readings done in large group situations, many discarnate spirits come through to communicate with specific sitters in attendance. It is interesting to get so many people from the other side visiting at the same time, and I often find myself in a much altered (not unpleasant) state of consciousness that is characterized by a sense of elation. This does happen in individual sittings, but most often not to the same extent. In a later chapter I will give specific examples of readings that involved immediate confirmation of accuracy and relevance.

I have always been a little uneasy about using the label "medium" to describe myself and, by extension, what I do. As far as the Spiritualist Church believes, no one can call themselves a medium who has not been certified in that church to be a medium. This requires that one become a reverend in the church, something I was not inclined to do since I have always been interested in visiting, i.e., walking in the shoes of, a religion while being reluctant to join any particular one. Plus, I do not believe that talking to and hearing from spirits, or practicing any other of the psychic abilities needs to be attached to a particular religion. The spirit, whether incarnate or discarnate, does not rely on religion to establish or fortify its existence. Again, I have never, in fact, spoken with any spirit who even brings up his or her religion when they were on the physical plane. I can usually ascertain something about it from the sitter's vibrations, but the discarnate spirit never mentions seeing any particular Master of any particular religion.

Actually, we can also consider two incarnate people speaking with each other. The topic of religious affiliation is not necessary in order to communicate. Yet, in reality, these spirits are speaking, albeit from the confines of a physical body. The same paradigm is true of spirit not so confined.

I have recently come to believe that what I do is akin to a translator or maybe a better analogy would be a telegraph operator who is able to decipher the dots and dashes of Morse code. I think a better label (though I remain far from believing I need one) is Spirit Communication Facilitator, which while it describes what I do, is still a little long for my liking. Perhaps Facilitator would be fine on its own. Spirit Intuitive is the descriptive I most often use because it suggests that I discern both incarnate and discarnate spirit.

How do we do it? How to we perceive through extra-sensory perception? Through the willful suspension of disbelief. There is the sensation of seeing what "is not there" and hearing "what cannot be heard."

Sometimes the images and sounds certainly seem tangible enough that I feel as though the image or sound is being processed through my physical eyes and ears, and other times it is less solid than the first wisps of a just-beginning-to-boil kettle.

Over time, different labels of cognitive abilities have become accepted as ways of describing what these "senses" do and how they work. While these labels sound highly esoteric and mystical, they are of a much simpler nature than they may seem.

There are four primary means of gathering information above and beyond the five physical senses. These include clairaudience, clairsentience, clairvoyance, and claircognizance.

Clairaudience, or clear hearing, allows the hearing of sounds both apparently internal and external. Throughout time, there are many reports of people hearing sounds that have no physical origin. In the Bible, Abraham and Moses, among many others, are reported to have heard the spoken words of God, or that entity that is larger than our individual selves, but the average person may be able to hear spirits, or their guides. An interesting phenomenon that many have experienced, including myself, is hearing celestial music, a sound that seems to emanate from the skies and the planets. It is a very beautiful, ethereal sound, more akin to the best "new age" music than classical music. Many people have experienced hearing their name called when no one physical is there. This sound may originate from spirit space. One famous example of clairaudience is the case of Joan of Arc, who reports having heard the voices of angels, guiding her to free France from English domination. As one may note from her trial and execution, hearing voices and admitting to it can sometimes be a dangerous activity. A related phenomenon is known as Electronic Voice Phenomena, or EVP, which is the recording of spirit voices or music when there is no physical means of producing the sound present. The sounds are not heard physically during the recording process, but are present on the recording mechanism when played back. For me, with my weak comfort level with technology, this is a disconcerting method of spirit communication.

Clairsentience is also known as clear sensing, and involves perception of non-physical stimuli associated with all other sensing other than hearing and sight. Under this category would fall, for example, the perception of odors that are not physically there. Many people report detecting the aroma of roses when none are present. It is often spirit announcing their presence to a loved one through the only sense available to them, i.e., the incarnate person is acknowledged as a person who would not enjoy or accept any other mode of spirit communication. I believe that intuition falls into this category and that topic will be dealt with in a later chapter.

The most well-known psychic sense is clairvoyance, or clear seeing. Most mediums also identify themselves as clairvoyants, as the former really only refers to spirit communication, while clairvoyance includes the extra-sensory perception of other stimuli. Examples of this include prophetic visions and seeing pictures or items one does not have immediate access to. For example, when I attended an Association for Research and Enlightenment (ARE) seminar in Virginia, we were asked to draw a picture of a photo in a sealed envelope that was held up in the front of the room. As I perceived it, the photo seemed composed of circles and cones and rectangular columns. I drew these shapes as I saw them, and the picture I created did indeed abstractly reflect the shapes of the enveloped photo of a circus scene.

Claircognizance, or clear knowing, is the gaining of information other than from some recognizable source. There is a great controversy over prayer in the schools, but I maintain there always was and always will be prayer in schools, especially during exams. Sometimes I would sit absolutely stymied by a question the answer to which I had not a clue. Suddenly information that seemed relevant to the question would flow into my head and I would use it, often finding out later that I had, indeed supplied (or, rather, been supplied with) the correct answer. A lot of mediumistic ability relies on this clear knowing with information being passed through the modes of seeing and hearing, resulting in knowledge beyond the physical input of these senses.

Claircognizance is also the extra-sensory ability that most sustains intuition—knowing what one cannot possibly know by any other means.

Other modes of extra sensory perception include precognition and psychometry. As the name implies, precognition is knowing before an event or action that it will take place. This is what a vast majority of people who visit psychics and mediums want; they want to know what is going to happen in their future. Unfortunately, a psychic or medium can only relate to a sitter what they are perceiving at that moment. Once that moment passes, future events may change or a sitter may take a different direction than the one the medium perceived during the reading. Thus, any prediction has limited reliability and freewill is still the paramount factor in how one's life will play out. I tell a sitter that any predictive information needs to be viewed in these terms. Although there are certain life lessons we have incarnated to learn, we also have the ability to make decisions and change the day-to-day movement of our lives.

Psychometry is a method of tuning into and focusing on the vibration of the sitter in order to gain access to their discarnate loved one(s) and/or information about the sitter him/herself. This technique involves holding an item, preferably a piece of jewelry worn frequently by the sitter. This method is also often used in cases of missing people. An item the person owned is presented to the psychic and he or she is able to sense the vibration of the person from the item. Criminal cases have been known to have been solved in this manner using the information the psychic is able to provide.

In one instance, during an individual reading, I held the ring of the sitter's mother who had passed. The sitter was having a hard time coping with her mother's transition. I did not know to whom the ring belonged. The mother gave specific information so the daughter could identify her, including showing me an ornate wrought iron wall hanging that I could not understand, but that the daughter recognized immediately.

Just to clarify, a medium generally receives the majority of information from a particular spirit or spirits, although most mediums are also psychic, so they are able to access pertinent information using clairaudience, clairvoyance, telepathy, intuition, etc. The first reading I ever received and the first reading I gave both relied on the connection created through psychometry.

As mentioned previously, I attended college and lived in Fredonia, New York, for a few years. About 9 miles down the road is the spiritualist community of Lily Dale. There, one can find a town built on the premise that "there is no death, there are no dead." Lily Dale was first established in 1879 as a center for spiritual development and a residential community for the Spiritualist Church. It sits on the shore of Cassadaga Lake and includes a beautiful old-growth forest in which one can find Inspiration Stump where message services are held. The rough paved roads weave between Victorian cottages that have seen better days, but are still reminiscent of a time when Lily Dale was a place that many people visited. It is believed that such notables visited Lily Dale as Mahatma Gandhi, Sir Arthur Conan Doyle, Mae West, Franklin and Eleanor Roosevelt, Leo Tolstoy's daughter Russian Countess Alexandra Tolstoy, Harry Houdini, and Susan B. Anthony. The summer months still buzz with the excitement of visitors who come to attend services and get readings.

The home of the Fox sisters, whose mediumistic rappings helped to promote the establishment of Spiritualism in America in the 1800s, was moved to the Dale in 1916, though unfortunately it burned to the ground in 1955. The Fox sisters, who were variously praised as gifted and condemned as charlatans, originally lived in Hydesville, New York. They psychically detected the bones of a peddler who had been murdered and buried in the basement of their home. His bones were found behind a wall there and put on display when the house was moved to Lily Dale. Many celebrities believed in the abilities of the sisters including P.T. Barnum, William Cullen Bryant, James Fenimore Cooper, and newspaper editor Horace Greeley.

One must be a certified medium to own property in Lily Dale. As in any profession, there have always been those mediums who are quite simply amazing in their ability to look onto a person's life path and show them the future (keeping in mind the caveat previously mentioned regarding the limitations of accuracy when freewill is involved). Then there are others who, although certified, fall into the classification of weakly connected. My children and I joke that people of that ilk tend to give readings that go something like: "I see you have a mother, and she is older than you." The problem is knowing which medium is which, and, even harder, which of the better ones might be having an off day (it happens) or simply can not connect to the sitter (it also happens, especially when the sitter is less than cooperative).

I wish I could remember exactly how it came to pass that I had my first reading ever, and that this first reading was with Gladys DeChard, one of the best mediums I have ever encountered. The reading was done at the end of 1973, or perhaps the beginning of 1974. I believe an acquaintance on the Fredonia campus set up the reading and drove me over to the community. Now, remember, I had been aware of spirit since I was a little girl, so I was more curious than anything else, having never had a reading before, except for a palm reader at a high school fair who told me I would live a long time and have several husbands.

I knocked on the door of her cottage and was ushered into a small sitting area. She was a psychometrist also, and asked for an article to hold. I gave her my rose cameo ring that I had worn for years. Rather than contact any of my relatives, I believe now she was in communication with her own guides. She told me I would meet someone with blond hair and blue eyes on

February 5, 1974, and that we would start a relationship on February 14. She went on to say we would be engaged on May 3 of that year, and other details too numerous to mention. Suffice it so say that every event this woman predicted came true on the dates she indicated. The timeframe was well beyond the norm, and incidents that she predicted continued for almost three years, oftentimes with a great deal of pain, since there were several break-ups and reconciliations over that time. In the end, the young man and I married in 1976, and divorced in 1977. Sometime before the marriage, I went back to visit Mrs. DeChard. She took my ring, looked me in the eye, and reminded me I had freewill to change the path, to alter the coming events. I told her I felt I had to see it through to the end. She shook her head, sighing at my youthful stubbornness.

Since that time, I have never had so accurate a reading, but if I had, and I had been warned about the future as she had warned me, I would have, through the discernment gained through experience, perhaps chosen different decisions, thus altering the path. Again, as I write that, I know that it not quite true, because everything that would or could have been changed would have or could have changed my current life, which I would not wish to change at all. I guess the most important thing to keep in mind is that each decision constitutes a crap shoot, or, more accurately, a spin of the roulette wheel, except rather than trying to predict where the ball will land, it is often necessary, in a well-examined life, to guess what will be the result of changing one's path. Socrates said, "The unexamined life is not worth living." I agree with this whole-heartedly . . . we must always be aware of the possible ramifications of our actions and steps, not only on our own lives, but also on the lives of others.

In the mid-1970s, I also gave my first reading. It was to a security guard where I worked. He was a wreck from not sleeping and needed to take a great deal of prescribed Valium (which is used to alleviate anxiety and insomnia) in order to even begin to approach a state of calm. Knowing of my interest and involvement in paranormal work, he asked me if I would give him a reading. I was reluctant at first. I could sense that this man needed more help than I could, or should, probably give him, but I felt Roger nudge me into doing the reading, and I took the man's ruby and gold ring in my hand. Immediately, I wish I could fling it into a nearby field. It seemed to contain the most discomforting vibrations of anything I had ever held.

I told him the ring had had three previous owners, which he confirmed. I told him that these owners had been relatives and all three were now deceased. Again, he said that this was true. I then told him that one person had drowned, the next had been hit by a train, and the third had had a massive heart attack. He confirmed that these, indeed, were
the manners in which all three had passed over. I need to remind you, this was my FIRST reading and I was definitely confused by this ability and filled with quite a bit of trepidation, since I was still holding the ring with the strangely awful vibrations emanating from it into the palm of my hand.

I knew that I was being helped with this reading (how could I be making this stuff up if, indeed, it was all true?). With that sense of confidence, and an authority I didn't know I had, I told him he should get rid of the ring and when he did, he would begin to feel better and be able to give up the Valium and get some sleep. He said he would think about it.

Shortly after that, I stopped working there and didn't see the man for several months. When I did, he looked like a new man. He told me that he had disposed of the ring and had begun to feel better almost immediately. He was off the Valium and sleeping well. He thanked me, but I was also grateful, to him and to spirit.

I never did a lot of readings in Fredonia, although there was one time when I went back to visit some friends and ended up sitting in a circle in the living room of one of them and ended up doing 16 "mini" readings, one right after the other of people I barely knew. I seemed to have a reasonable rate of accuracy, and everyone was pleased with the readings. What one fellow didn't know was that I determined he was a closeted gay man and rather than reveal his private matters in such a public setting, I refrained from sharing this information. It was later, when I could speak to him alone, that I told him what I had sensed. Although chagrined at my awareness, he confirmed that what I had perceived was indeed true.

The desire to contact spirit and to predict the future is as old as our need to incarnate. I believe there was a time when we all lived on the spirit plane, which was then, of course recognized as "the only place there was to be." In order to gain experience and to allow the spirit to grow, the opportunity to slow down the vibrations to the physical level was presented by those of a higher vibrational level than the one on which we all lived. It is hard, while we sit in the physical, to contemplate that there is a spirit plane, let alone from here and from there, to consider that there are infinitely higher planes to which we may aspire and/or may simply experience.

On the next spirit (i.e., non-physical) plane, we did not experience the differences that inform our physical lives. We enter our bodies as pure spirit, ready to experience whatever we have decided to on this plane: we are of a race, a skin color, an ethnic group, a socio-economic basis, male or female, and any other number of attributes available through a physical existence. When we pass from this plane, though, we now take this new expression with us and it becomes a part of our spirit and a part, then, of our spirit group, which then has the opportunity to reincarnate together in new circumstances from which to gain knowledge, and one would hope, wisdom.

For example, a nuclear family grouping, consisting of a mother, father, two male and two female siblings might decide to experience an incarnation in Rochester, NY. Each person comes to the incarnated state from a previous lifetime in which the father, for example, may have taken on the role of one of the daughters in the group, or a cousin, or a close friend. Each change in relationship dynamic, created by taking on different roles, leads to a greater knowledge and awareness of self and self in the group dynamic, both of which help to provide growth on this and other planes.

This act of incarnating repeatedly with generally the same group of people, as family, as friends, as acquaintances, gives, to varying degrees, a sense of familiarity. It is this that accounts for those moments when upon meeting someone for the first time, there is a recognition of something familiar about that person. Perhaps this also helps to explain love at first sight, as two soul mates once again find each other, or loathing at first sight, as two adversaries encounter each other once more face to face.

All of this is understandable only if we hold the idea of spirit in mind. It is the truth inherent in our acceptance of our true being as spirit that allows us to recognize each other and to communicate, as Mary Martin implied, without being dependent on words. It is how we exist as our true selves, as spirit bound together with the purpose of learning, loving, and growing as a vast community, whether incarnate, or discarnate, because surely not all of our soul group must incarnate at the same time. Of course, as we leave our bodies, some of this group is incarnate and some discarnate and the communication is still available to all of us, in whatever state in which we find ourselves. And it is this ability to communicate, to sense the similar spirit nature of each other, that will eventually lead us home to a place of understanding and peace. And it is this ability to communicate that allows mediums to act as facilitators between those who need help seeing and hearing spirit and their discarnate loved ones.

Chapter 4

The Gift of Communication:
Serving as a Conduit

We are all connected to everyone and everything in the universe. Therefore, everything one does as an individual affects the whole. All thoughts, words, images, prayers, blessings, and deeds are listened to by all that is.
(Serge Kahili King)

The reason we are able to communicate with spirit, and experience moments of the best and most productive communication between those incarnate, is because we are all of the same essential matter and that matter is a part of an interconnected web of existence, whether we are in or out of the physical plane. In fact, this web supersedes the various planes of reality and lies at the foundation of our oneness. We are, indeed, "all connected to everyone and everything in the universe."

When a medium prepares for a reading, the focus is on opening his or her faculties in order to perceive whatever information is forthcoming in whatever mode it is communicated. Some mediums have elaborate tablecloths and objects that are sacred to them. Although I have performed readings without any preparation whatsoever, I admit to feeling more secure when I have lit a white candle and quickly asking that only positive energies and beings come in to visit. The white candle seems to help set the environment so that negative and elemental beings are reluctant to cause havoc. I also like to have a crystal, usually clear quartz, to help as both a grounding for me, a focus for both my personal physical and spirit being, and as an amplifier of the energies coming through.

When a sitter comes in, we get comfortably seated and then I can feel a slight shift in perception, a small alteration in which I feel less physical and can allow my spirit to have a stronger presence. Thus, a reading on my side of things is both mental and not mental at the same time. Physically, the sensation of perceiving spirit and information is primarily from the top of my forehead to a little below eye-level. As the reading progresses, the sense of my physical being ebbs and sometimes I am no longer fully aware of my body, though this does not happen very often.

Sometimes the spirit the sitter wishes to communicate with comes right in, and sometimes other spirits make their presence known first. By using psychometry, and holding an item belonging to the sitter, or to the individual in spirit, I am able to establish a link between me, the sitter, and the loved one in spirit. Once in a great while, no spirit comes forth for the sitter, and if that is the main purpose of his or her visit, I end the reading, though most people insist I tell them something and then I have to rely on Roger and other spirits who come in and tell the sitter what they want or need to hear.

One of the hardest kinds of readings to give is when the sitter comes in stoically and refuses to show any facial expression or confirmation (or denial) of any kind. Some skeptics believe mediums are actually only reading the facial expressions and body language of the sitter in order to gain information, but I think this is a silly notion. The name of a spirit named Joe, for example, is not going to manifest in my mind because of the way the person across from me is physically presenting themselves, and yet such specifics often are communicated during a reading. It is much more comfortable for me, and ultimately more informative for the sitter, to know that I am on the right track, and that the information means something to the sitter, and not that some other spirit is passing through and making themselves known who has no relationship to the sitter whatsoever. While I request that a sitter only give me yes or no indications until it is clearly established that I have made contact with the spirit they wish to speak to, having no response whatsoever can cause the individual in spirit to become frustrated also, and leave. Once the sitter and I both know I have the correct person in spirit, the reading often becomes more a conversation or transfer of information or a question and answer session, with me acting as facilitator and the incarnate and discarnate individuals often discussing things I do not understand at all.

To give you an idea of how some readings are conducted, I will share a few with you. These are selected from a journal I sometimes keep of readings that stand out because of their accuracy or oddness.

I read for a woman of Italian heritage. Her husband came through, also her great uncle or grandfather Dominick, aka Domi, who gave her an alabaster egg and a dove. She cried when her husband came through although I didn't know till the end it was her husband.

A woman and her two daughters came to hear from two relatives. One was Brian, the other was one woman's father-in-law. Brian had been in the service. I got the impression they had come on this particular day because it was an anniversary (of his death?). The father-in-law showed me a metal box full of his things. The daughter-in-law recognized it; she had it in her possession. Also, there was someone else who spoke of a legal paper (a will? a deed?) that needed to be looked at ASAP. They understood what I was talking about.

Now, that is one of the borderline frustrating aspects of giving readings of this nature. Oftentimes information is given and the readers thoroughly understand it, and confirm they understand it, and don't tell me what it is they understand. I still accept it as confirmation that I have reached the correct discarnate spirit for the sitter(s), but I never quite know what it is I have said to them.

I was booked for a gig at Rochester Institute of Technology during an on-campus information weekend for prospective students. There were several readers and it would involve a series of readings of 10 minutes in duration each. While it is challenging to do this kind of work, the progression of spirits moving through my space is exhilarating. For one woman, I identified by name her grandmother Marie, and for another, her grandma Rose; I identified another woman's best friend, who was out in the hallway, out of my line of sight, as Cassie/Cassandra. The oddest and yet most complete reading was for an African American student. The gentleman in spirit who came through came to America from Italy and was the cook in the family. And he was white. I truly did not see how this could be a relation of the young man in front of me, but I described the spirit nonetheless. The sitter broke out into an effusive grin. "That's my grandpa," he proclaimed, apparently pleased with his reading. Even when it seems as if there is nothing about the spirit that seems to relate to the sitter, I have learned to share the information and impressions I receive, and normally, the sitter joyfully acknowledges and confirms my communication.

On another occasion at NTID (the National Technical Institute for the Deaf, which is a part of RIT), I gave readings to deaf students. This was particularly interesting and challenging because I needed to use a sign-language interpreter in order to communicate with the students. Despite the difficulty in direct communication with the students, the readings went quite well except for when, periodically, I would slip up and start reading the interpreter instead of the sitter.

I had an appointment with a woman named Gloria and her daughter Gina. When they walked into the store, a man in spirit entered after them, said he was Frank and he was for them, and told me "let's get going." As soon as we started the reading, I told Gloria that Frank had come in with her. Yes, that was her husband's name. They had been married for 52 years. Frank had died in the past year on Christmas Eve. Frank came through as of Italian-descent, and a builder (he was a mason). He started to sing an Italian aria, and I told Gloria and Gina. Yes, indeed, he loved Italian opera. Frank showed me papers regarding land and I shared that. While they understood this, it also came back to them at a future reading. Frank was accompanied by a son in spirit who had died very young. He identified other family members, both incarnate and discarnate, and Gloria and Gina confirmed them all. I suddenly saw Frank in a military uniform and shared this with his family members. I didn't recognize the uniform; it looked different from the USA uniforms I was familiar with. Gloria and Gina confirmed that he had been in the Armed Forces in Italy. While I was reading for Gloria, I was shown her still incarnate 93-year old father. While he was very spry, he was also experiencing some issues related to being in such advanced age and alone, although I was shown that he was surrounded by people at his church. Apparently he lived at a distance and Gloria wanted him to come live closer to her, but this would be a problem because he was very close to and dependent on the people at his church.

Frank also indicated that there was going to be a problem with selling the land he had had as an investment. Gloria was dealing with the sale on the following Wednesday, and Frank told her there was a problem with a number, it had been transposed and needed to be rechecked.

Then I read the daughter, Gina. Frank talked about her low self-esteem and the need to follow her path more. He also told me her marriage was not going so well. She confirmed these reference points. Frank told me to tell Gina her soul mate would be coming in the next 4–6 years. He also showed me she had a 17-year old son who was interested in architecture and landscaping with bricks. Again Gina confirmed this and said he seemed to get his talent from his grandfather, i.e., Frank. At this point Frank wanted Gina to know that there were angels around her home watching over her.
In a subsequent reading on with Gloria, Albert, her grandfather, came in during the reading, and I got the Al part of his name.

A woman named Jenny, who was approximately 21 or 22, came in for a reading. While she did not have a specific spirit help with the reading, I still was able to discern a fair amount of information. When she sat down, she said she was named for her grandmother or great grandmother (she wasn't sure which). The name Brian came to me quite strongly and she confirmed that he was her boyfriend, whose mother another reader was reading at the same time. I became aware of the death of two boys in her high school class in a car accident. I also identified an incarnate friend of hers who had MS and a spirit came in to say there could be a cure in 1–2 years involving a mylar/teflon substance (please know that time is hard to pin down in readings but I hope that this cure is realized soon). I became aware that Jenny had taken trips to Spanish-speaking countries, and she said she had been to Costa Rica and plans to go to Mexico. I saw that she would eventually be visiting Spain on business. I saw that she was in college and she then told me that she was a Spanish major. I saw her tutoring a housebound 8th grader in the coming year, and she confirmed that she had tutored in the past. She indicated that she was impressed by my accuracy. I told her she had known since 7th grade her direction in life. I also told her that her boyfriend Brian was going to go to RIT for some sort of computer training and she said he wants to pursue architecture, and I said it was CAD (Computer-aided design) technology, which, as one less than knowledgeable with techie things, I recognized as information coming from spirit.

I read for a woman named Paula who is a friend of Gina's (Frank's daughter). I told her I sensed that her boyfriend was small, dark, and handsome and mistakenly thought his name was Greg, but it was John. I told her he seems to be getting a divorce, which she confirmed. I saw her and his 18-year old daughter shopping together. Spirit told me to tell her that John needed to check under the siding near the kitchen. She said she was drawn to 11:11 and also 3:11. Then her mother came through from spirit. She showed me an M, and Paula said it was for Mary (her grandmother) and mother (May was her middle name). I said her mom said that 3:11 was a strong connection between them. Paula said her mom died on 3/11. Her mom had me tell her that that was "their" time to be together now. I told Paula the 11:11 was her call to meditate/pray for world love and peace. I told her to keep a journal and she said she does.

In a reading with a woman, a young man in his late 30s/early 40s came in and told me to tell her that he was not in as much pain as everyone thought he was when he passed over and he wanted her to tell everyone else who was there when he passed that he was fine now and pain free. He showed me a garden of gourds and told me to tell the woman (who is his sister-in-law). I was reluctant to do so, because it seemed like such a strange image. He insisted and I shared this information with her. She told me his wife has a garden full of gourds. Subsequently, I gave a reading to a woman named Amy, who was the woman who had the gourd garden. It was her sister who had come in previously. While I was reading Amy (and wondering about how hard it might be to grow a gourd garden and how many people actually grew gourd gardens), her husband's stepfather, David came in and I described him. Apparently, he had died the previous Thursday. Her husband, Brian, has passed away two months earlier, after having fought leukemia for three years. Both David and Brian were excellent communicators and it was quite enjoyable to meet them, albeit from the non-physical world in which they now live.

Jean came in for a reading. She wanted to speak with her mother who recently had died suddenly of an aneurism. I could see her mother in a large dark box, and not opening her eyes to see where she was. I told Jean her belief system was so ingrained, she couldn't see past it (and her Dad was/is also in this condition). It is my understanding that one sees what one believes one will see when he/she transitions, so some people are left in this darkness until other spirits get them to open their eyes. Fred, Jean's mother's father in spirit, came through and said he knew now the beliefs he had taught her were/are wrong and he had been trying to get through to her, but she was quite stubborn. Jean corroborated the mis-beliefs and her mother's stubbornness. Her mother's brother-in-law, also in spirit, stopped in. He can't get through to her mother either. Roger, my guide, told me there would be an occasion for celebration coming up and (responding silently to Roger) I suggested wine and cheese, but Roger said no, she can't have cheese, and I related to Jean this silent conversation, and she said that was all quite true, and she could not have cheese.

A woman came in and gave no hint of whom she was trying to contact. The name Timothy came across clearly from the other side as a man appeared. Spirit normally appears behind and to the right or left of the sitter. He mentioned mushrooms and also showed me his "weird" feet that seemed to be able to turn beyond the point most people can turn their feet. The woman gasped and began to cry. She confirmed this information and said it was her husband (he loved mushrooms, and, indeed, his feet could turn as I was seeing them). I told her I sensed it had been a very sudden passing and she said he had died immediately from a heart attack. I was reluctant to share the next bit of information, but I have gotten myself into trouble by not sharing everything so I told the woman that her husband was indicating that not only did he have a propensity for childish behavior, so did she. She broke into a teary grin and confirmed this too. The two of them often found themselves acting in the most childish (not childlike, she assured me) manner. She complained that despite her best efforts, she was unable to sense him or hear him herself. This happens sometimes. The thing one wants most from spirit is the one thing that either the incarnate spirit is unable to perceive, the discarnate spirit is unable to communicate, or some combination of both. Her husband told me to tell her to sit quietly in their special place with a glass of white wine (apparently a wine they both enjoyed) and he would be there. He assured me he would do his best to reach out and make her feel his presence. I shared all this, and she left much comforted and hopeful.

During one of the strangest readings I have ever given, I told a young woman that a man close to her had recently died, and she confirmed that an older gentleman who was a neighbor of hers had passed that week. I saw him as a man in his mid to late 30s. Spirit normally appears first as they were at the end of life and then they take on the physical appearance they most liked of themselves in the physical life just passed, normally in their 20s or 30s. I told her he seemed to like gardening, especially herbs, and preferred using a trowel to a shovel so he could be "hands on." He focused on the image of gardening for a bit, and then also showed me water and a canoe, both elements she confirmed. I am not sure what made me ask, but I asked her when he had died and what street they lived on. She gave me both bits of information and I recognized the street as one near the high school I had attended. Although I never would ask such a question, I felt compelled to ask the man's name, which he had not given to me directly. She told me and it turned out that he was a member of the choir I had recently left and I had gone to school with his daughter. This was the very first time I had done a reading for someone else in which I knew the person in spirit. He was a very special man and known for his generous spirit. The sitter and I both shed some tears at realizing we both knew this man and how much he would be missed from this plane by so many people.

Just so that you understand that communicating with people and beings on other dimensions does not necessarily give me great wisdom, insight, or understanding, it was not until I wrote the previous paragraph that it occurred to me: the gentleman in spirit kept reiterating his love for and involvement with gardening. Once I was aware of who I was in contact with, I should have seen immediately his use of the homophone (or near homophone). In this life he had a wry sense of humor and enjoyed turns of language. The reason for my astonishment so long after the reading? The gentleman's last name was Gardner, so very similar to gardener, apparently his favorite hobby!

In addition to individual readings, I frequently am called upon to help with séances during which another medium, Char Hacker, and I give messages from those in spirit to the ten or so incarnate individuals gathered in a circle around a table that holds lit candles and, often incense. Séances are especially fun for me to take part in because there are so many people in spirit that come to see their loved ones that it often takes on an air of celebration, though not all the messages are positive.

At a recent séance, a woman sat down next to me who had obviously had a drink before coming to the store (the séances are held at Psychic's Thyme, a New Age bookstore in Rochester, NY). At first I was a bit disconcerted, because alcohol tends to lower the vibrations in the room. Fortunately, the odor dissipated quickly as, I assume, did her "buzz." Suddenly, I was aware of an overwhelming odor of alcohol coming from behind her. It was a gentleman whom she identified as her father, who had had a drinking problem in life. He told me to tell her she needed to get her act together because she was beginning to take risks with alcohol and things could end quite badly for her. She started crying and told me that she had been stopped recently for driving under the influence. Her father had me make it quite clear that her behavior had to stop and that she should dedicate herself to going back to school, which she confirmed she was about to do.

During another séance, a discarnate man in military dress from the Vietnam War came into the circle and slowly walked around, looking closely at each face. Finally, he turned to me and said the person he had come to see was not there. I apologized and said I had no control over who showed up and that I was sorry he had come and been disappointed. He left, shaking his head sadly.

Several weeks later, we held another séance. An acquaintance of mine who worked at the store was there with his partner, Chuck. As the séance progressed, the spirit from the Vietnam War came in again, walked around looking at the people sitting in the circle, and stopped in front of Chuck. "He's here this time," he said gratefully. He placed his hands on Chuck's shoulders and brought his face close to his. I told Chuck what was happening and it seemed that he was aware that the soldier was near him. I told him that the man, who Chuck identified as Wayne, his first partner, had died of something other an accident. Chuck confirmed this . . . Wayne had died of AIDS and had been 23 years older than Chuck. Wayne was very glad to see Chuck, who, apparently, was supposed to have been at the earlier séance, but at the last minute was unable to attend!

I have always been aware of spirits and able to communicate with them without much fuss, muss, or ado, but some mediums are more comfortable serving spirit from a trance state, in which the medium slides over, so-to-speak, and allows spirit to "do the driving," i.e., be in control of the proceedings. I believe it would be similar to driving down the road and losing track of the distance traveled. One moment you are at the store, and the next you are home, without much conscious thought of how you got there, simply because (variances in weather conditions taken into account) you have made the journey so many times, it is like second nature to you. You do not need to think: turn right, drive one mile, turn left, turn into the driveway. You simply do these motions and end up where you are supposed to be. A trance medium also does not need to give conscious thought to what is going on during the trance-state, although the medium can easily be thought of as an on-looker, watching the spirit driving. When you are driving without thinking about it, you are still thinking about something, though perhaps not the driving you are doing at that moment. The medium allows his or her thoughts to be filled with those of the spirit she or he has contacted, but normally speaks with her or his own voice, and is aware of the speaker and what is being said, for the most part, though this depends on the level of trance in which the medium finds him or herself.

In my case, while I do not believe I do readings from discarnate beings to incarnate beings in a state of trance, I have entered into a separate, heightened state of consciousness in which (or from which) I am able to access higher information that comes out as a stream-of-consciousness discourse. The topic areas always seem to be about matters of existence, the validity of spirit (incarnate and discarnate), and other esoteric matters. Primarily it happens when I am trying to teach someone or impart some knowledge to them that I know I know, but have never actually articulated before. I often get to the end of one of these discourses and wish I had had a tape recorder going, and instead I have to scramble to lock the thoughts on paper, and ask whomever I have been speaking to for help in recreating the information.

It is my awareness that this information comes from those considered Master Teachers who are found on different planes of incarnate and discarnate existence. Master Teachers do, indeed, incarnate on Earth and these have included Buddha and Jesus, for example, and many more unknown but who have walked among us, imparting universal wisdom. More Master Teachers are to be found on discarnate and non-carnate planes, the latter meaning in forms that have never inhabited a three-dimensional body. Whenever I receive information from Master Teachers, there is a feeling slightly less corporeal, as though my spirit is filling more of my body and emanating beyond the bounds of my skin. As I indicated, the information I receive always seems to be in answer to some question that may not have been articulated.

I remember once, a long time ago, having a "dream" that was strikingly vivid of sitting on a verdant hillside in the presence of a Master Teacher clothed in glowing white robes who was teaching some sort of Master Class, as there were others in attendance. To this day, the image remains especially vivid and while the imparted information seems forgotten on a conscious level, I know the lessons remain a part of my body of knowledge.

At the deepest level of trance, where to the best of my knowledge I have never gone, a medium can serve as a channel, which goes beyond sliding over, and instead actually allows for the voice of the spirit to come through via the vocal cords of the channeler. The medium relinquishes control not only of his or her voice, but body as well. While this is not possession as it is thought of in the popular culture (because there is an agreement between the channel and the spirit that does not exist in cases of possession), it does involve the spirit slipping on the coat of the incarnate person and using their body to communicate with others. The body of the medium takes on facial expressions and mannerisms of the spirit to the point where sitters are not aware of the incarnate person before them at all and, rather, perceive the spirit communicating. A channel medium can either work with one spirit or allow him or herself to be a physical conduit for different spirits, in other words, whomever comes knocking. I have seen film of a famous channeling medium and I am still not sure what to make of it. While on the one hand it has the potential for demonstrating that the body is but a shell, a protective casing for the spirit, and one could come and go as one pleased while keeping the body alive, it also has the potential for great misuse.

One can call oneself a channel and may be hooking up with a spirit, maybe even a Master Spirit, and develop a following. But just as people on this plane are not always available for a conversation, so too are those in non-physical planes of existence not always available. When one has reserved space and charged money, one must produce what the people have paid for, and if that entity should not happen to be available at that moment, I am afraid it opens the door for some unpleasant stop-gap measures to be pursued, e.g., recreating a previous situation during which the spirit was available. While I am sure there are many fine channeling mediums, I admit I have issues with the attendant dramatics that seem so prevalent in this manner of communicating. Also, it tends to make it one of those "I am special and you are not" kinds of abilities, which should not be the case at all when those of us incarnate wish to communicate with those discarnate. I like to think of the process as simply picking up the phone and speaking with the person, or sitting down for a cup of coffee with them, rather than some involved and complicated process.

I like to think that my belief in the very real simple nature of communicating with spirit will eventually, when we have all grown sufficiently, be the norm, and we will give no more thought to having a conversation with Aunt Mary after she transitions than before that process takes place. We are all spirit, experiencing various degrees of solidity or manifestation, and if we could all keep that in mind, there would be a lot less fear in the world, and the sorts of behaviors that fear elicits—violence, war, etc.

Sometimes, I am not so much a conduit as I am a recipient. Such is the case in my encounter with a young man named John E. Hart.

I had gone to the emergency room of Dunkirk Hospital, the nearest one to Fredonia, with severe abdominal pains. I was placed on a gurney in the emergency examination room, but before anyone could examine me, there was a great commotion. They wheeled someone into the bay next to mine and just before someone thought to close the curtain between us, I made out that this person was male and his knee looked as though someone had chopped out a 90° wedge from it. The staff worked rapidly and suddenly I became aware that they were draining his lungs into a glass container that happed to be on my side of the room. That is when my desire to leave the room became greater than the pain in my stomach. I gingerly moved myself to the waiting room.

As I sat there, deciding I was feeling much better and wanting to leave the hospital entirely, the staff quickly rolled the young man past me and into a waiting ambulance for the trip to Buffalo. They could do no more for him at their small hospital.

As you can imagine, this was quite upsetting to me and I sent out thoughts that he be helped. As I waited for the room to be cleaned so I could be examined, it could not have been more than 40 minutes later that they wheeled the man's body past me on the way to, I assume, the morgue. I was devastated that this person, who seemed to be around my age of 19 then, would have died so young.

After a quick examination that determined I was not in imminent danger, I went back to my apartment in Fredonia. At some point, I heard on the radio that the fellow's name was John E. Hart, that he was 19, and that, as he had walked on the side of a local road, a drunk driver had mowed him down.

The next day, my dad came from Rochester to bring me home to be examined by my own doctor. As I lay in my familiar bed in my family home, the door to my bedroom closed, I heard our dog Pippin making a strange sound from the other side of the door. I opened my eyes and before me was a gray, gelatinous figure, trying to gain recognizable form. I could hear him say, "It's okay. I'm free . . . it'll be all right . . . don't worry." With that, the form wafted towards the ceiling and disappeared, and Pippin ceased his eerie sound. I became very calm and relieved, understanding that this was John E. Hart, bringing me comfort and the knowledge that, indeed, he was all right.

Apparently, on his way to the next plane, John had felt my concern for him and made a stop to salve my spirit, which at that early date in my development, was sorely bruised from the events of the previous 24 hours.

Recently, a woman I had met previously and I were speaking after I had been writing at a favorite café, Java's, because there is a particularly nice set of vibrations there that are conducive for allowing the words to flow more freely onto the page. I mentioned this to the woman and she asked me what it feels like to hear and see spirit, what was the difference for me, what did it feel like. I realized that actually there isn't much of a difference from interacting with incarnate spirits and discarnate ones. I told her it is a matter of focus and attention. While I am talking with her, I may be paying attention to the words she is saying and maybe what she looks like and that she is paging through a magazine. If I were to shift my attention to someone else, perhaps at a nearby table, I would be noticing things about that person. I would see what they look like and perhaps hear snippets of a conversation they are having. If I excuse myself from the first woman, and move towards the second person and start talking with him or her, I will be communicating more closely and attentively with that person, leaving the woman to read her magazine. I explained to her that that is pretty much what I experience when I speak with someone in spirit . . . it is not so much a shift in awareness, though that is a result, as it is a shift in attention and focus. On the other hand, if I am receiving some sort of communication from a "higher" entity, i.e., a Master, and I am not simply communicating, but rather am learning something or being made to remember something, there is a definite shift in awareness. It is as though I am allowing the information to pass through me, not engaging in a conversation. On occasion, I am able to write down some of the knowledge that is being given to me. Frequently, this occurs when someone has asked me about how an esoteric matter works, e.g., some aspect of transition, or perhaps some global matter of import that I am discussing, and it just seems to start to flow in words that I do not feel I am selecting on my own.

When I serve as a medium, either in a reading with one or two other sitters, or in a séance with eight or more, the goal is always to present verifiable information from the discarnate plane in order to alleviate the fear of death and ease the pain of physical separation.

Chapter 5

The Gift of Healing:
Helping to Salve the Spirit

The fundamental delusion of humanity is to suppose that I am here and you are out there.
(Yasutani Roshi)

How do we heal each other and ourselves? Through the same mechanism of love and the conduit through which love flows. How do we use this knowledge of and this connection to spirit to grow within the interdependent web?

Everything and everyone contains energy. It is believed by many that this energy exists and functions in what are known as chakras, energy centers aligned down the core of the body, and along meridians that run throughout the body. There are many "alternative" healing and cleansing techniques that are becoming more widely accepted. These techniques help to clear blockages or interruptions in the energy flow, the result of which is known as disease or "dis-ease." Acupuncture, acupressure, Reiki, and other laying-on-of-hands techniques work with the energy, also known as ki or chi, to bring about healing.

The energy emanates from the body as an observable aura that can be successfully read by those so trained and can lead to diagnoses of illnesses. All energy therapies work with/on the energy fields around and in the body, which can be manipulated to facilitate healing by focusing the "universal life force" on the disease. The energy accessed in healing methodologies is a part of the universal interdependent web that connects all beings, whether incarnate or discarnate. It is the vital energy that helps to support the spirit, the soul, etc. This energy is what helps bind us together, one to the other.

In traditional Chinese medicine, illness occurs because of the improper flow of qi (life force) through the body. Balance, e.g., yin/yang, is missing and needs to be re-established through a variety of methods, including acupuncture, acupressure, herbal remedies, massage, and/or meditation. Acupuncture (using very fine needles) and acupressure (using the hands via pressure) stimulate the energy meridians flowing through the body, in conjunction with the charkas, to correct the improper flow of energy that causes disease.

Reiki (Japanese meaning Rei, higher power, and ki, life force energy), for example, taps into the universal life force energy and allows the healer, through his or her hands, to transmit that energy into the one seeking healing.

In addition, one can employ the methods inherent in the practice of feng shui to heal the personal environment in order to increase healthy energy flow and achieve balance. Feng shui seeks to create and maintain a balanced energy (chi) based on the concepts of yin (passive, female cosmic energy) and yang (active, male cosmic energy) by, for example, the arrangement of furniture and colors in an environment in order to permit the free flow of energy. A larger aspect of this would include recognizing the earth as a spiritual entity itself in need of healing that can be attained through an awareness found in the eco-spiritualist movement that is discussed in Chapter 10.

The use of crystals and stones in healing, especially of the chakras and energy meridians is a widely used healing method. The theory is that different crystals and stones contain different vibrational patterns based on their chemical composition. These energies interact with those within the body to facilitate healing and relief of physical disruptions. Another form of healing involves the human aura, various colored energies that flow around the human body. There are those who have the skill to see (clairvoyantly, not physically) and read the aura in order to detect illness and to recommend courses of action for healing.

Western forms of alternative or complementary methods of healing include meditation and biofeedback (which help to develop personal control over one's energies and healing properties by developing the ability to place the body in a state of balance), and hypnosis, which, whether performed by one skilled in the art or developed as a self-induced method, can lead to greater personal understanding and control of symptoms.

Hypnosis can also be a means to bringing incarnate spirits to remembrance of previous incarnations, reliving traumas that are contributing to dis-ease in the current incarnation and thus helping to release those by-gone situations and allowing healing to occur. Past-life regression, occurring via hypnotic inducement and suggestion, is becoming a more widespread healing modality.

When medical professionals work to heal a person, they are trying to fix a physical manifestation. If you break a leg, they set it and put it in a cast, and wait for it to mend. If you suffer a heart attack, they might try different courses of action to get the heart to beat regularly and maintain its intended function. If you have cancer, they remove and try to eradicate the errant cells that are causing the problem. The one thing most doctors do not do is check to determine if there is a non-physical component to the medical issue. While the pain of breaking a leg might not seem to be rooted in a non-physical problem, the amount of pain very well could be and even the fact that the leg has broken may be a sign of a deeper manifestation of dis-ease. Was this the point in this incarnation at which you decided to allow your leg to be broken in order to gain a certain perspective on the physical reality you are experiencing? Does breaking your leg at this particular moment bring you into contact with people with whom you share an inter-life bond? Or did breaking your leg cause someone totally new to come into your sphere? Did your need for help during the time of healing create a space in which others needed to experience compassion towards you? And at the same time, was there something to be gained by your opportunity to accept that compassion and help? Of course, it might be easier to understand this idea in relation to a cancer growing in the body.

In the instance of cancer, cells take on a manifestation that is not compatible with the human body, i.e., these cells become different from what would be considered normal in the body and, indeed, become invasively dangerous to the health of the body. This disruption in the individual cells (the cancerous cells) and to the neighboring healthy cells creates a situation of imbalance and discord. While this is the result, it may also be that imbalance and discord caused the situation in the first place. A disruption in energy, brought on by any number of internal and environmental causes can lead to this state of dis-ease. According to a fact sheet available at the National Cancer Institute's cancer.gov website:

> The complex relationship between physical and psychological health is not well understood. Scientists know that psychological stress can affect the immune system, the body's defense against infection and disease (including cancer); however, it is not yet known whether stress increases a person's susceptibility to disease (Segerstrom, S. and Miller, G., "Psychological stress and the human immune system: A meta-analytic study of 30 years of inquiry." *Psychological Bulletin* 2004; 130(4): 601–630).

While a direct correlation has yet to be scientifically proven, many acknowledge that stress can affect the immune system, opening us up to all sorts of illnesses and ailments. Employing meditation and stress-reducing techniques would help to alleviate the proclivity toward illness and dis-ease. Working to gain and maintain a state of physical, emotional, mental, and spiritual balance can help the individual to allow the flow of energies that promote good health.

The best physicians heal from and within a place of love. Theirs is a calling to help others by healing their physical ailments, but also, whether acknowledged consciously or not, through the healing aspect of love. When they set a broken bone, when they diagnose the common cold, when they suture a cut, when they work to eradicate the cancer, their hands do the physical work, but their hearts and spirits reach toward the heart and spirit of the patient, offering salve and solace to these aspects as well.

A healer who works primarily at the energy level, the heart/spirit level, seeks to discover the ailment, the disease, to put to rights the imbalance that is associated with that particular illness. Whole body healings are done for general wellness, but specific healings target specific locations and the healer works to remove the blockages and allow the energy to flow freely and healthily throughout the body. This healing has implications on both the physical and spiritual levels. Because it is based on the manipulation and transference of energy—the healer often is a conduit through which higher healing energies flow—it is not necessary for the healer to be in the presence of the one requiring intervention in order to effect a healing. Energy can be sent from the healer to the recipient through active visualization, seeing the person at a distance and sending healing to that person in the same way the healer would if the person were in the same room. This can involve visualizing one's hands emitting this energy and sending it over the illusion of time-space in order to effectuate healing.

We are all healers, whether we realize it or not. Every time we say gesundheit or bless you to someone who has just sneezed, we are sending healing to them. In the Bible, there is a story that tells that God blew the soul into Adam's nostril. And as far back as Ancient Greece, it was believed that when one sneezed, one's soul (or spirit) was blown out (and actually eventually departed for good through that route) and that saying bless you or gesundheit ensured that the soul would remain in the body.

Healing can also take place through prayer, wherein people (normally a group of two or more) ask for healing for a person. Usually, those praying do not consider their active role in the healing, but rather believe that God or a higher being is healing the person. While this may be partly true, it is also true that the act of two or more people sending healing love at the same time can aid in the healing, if not actually effectuate it in its entirety.

When the Master Jesus said, "When two or more are gathered in my name, there is love," as an enlightened being, he did not mean in his earthly name, Jesus, but in the name of his real existence, the spiritual reality. When we gather in spiritual connectivity, we generate a powerful force of love that is capable of healing and germinating all sorts of "miraculous" occurrences. We could heal each other, or heal the planet. Of course, a broken body or a broken earth requires physical intervention as well, but that intervention would then be sustained by the spiritual healing power transmitted through the healing energy of love.

The healing travels along the pathways of the interconnected web. That is what allows someone in Rochester, New York, to heal or help someone in Paris, France, or Kenya, or Tokyo. The love and healing flow like blood traveling through our bodies, nourishing our organs. Just as an energy blockage in the body causes dis-ease, so too does blockage in the interdependent web cause cosmic distress. Wherever we cease to tend to the needs of each other, or the planet, blockages and fissures are allowed to form, causing dis-ease to spirits on all planes. This leads to cosmic angst and a need to clear the blockage and bring balance back to the multi-realities in which we exist.

The 11:11 phenomenon is one way to bring together and focus energies for the common good. It is a call for whole segments of our earth's population to pray at the same time for general healing of each other and the earth and the cosmos and the entire interdependent web.

The 11:11 phenomenon (which will be discussed further in Chapter 10) allows us to pause during our day (at 11:11) to send out peace and love to each other across the interdependent web. Just stopping for the same minute during which others are stopping to send forth this powerful energy helps to connect us and to empower our thoughts and prayers for the greater good. The sending of healing at this time, for others as well as for the planet, can be magnified by the numbers of people stopping to do so.

Just as there are physicians who are called to heal the body, there are those who are called to heal the spirit in time of stress, duress, and/or sudden transitioning. When the call goes out along the spiritual plane that there is a need for the services of those both trained for such work and for those who are simply attuned to the need, there is a heightened sense of urgency and the undeniable need to respond. The extrasensory perceptions are awakened to a degree that, for example, one not only can see and hear the incidents creating the need, but there is a sense of being a firsthand witness to the unfolding events.

Washington, DC, is beautiful in the snow. The monuments on the Mall take on an ethereal presence, silently bearing witness to the passing of time, power, and pomp. Being a transplant from the harsher environs of Rochester, NY, I didn't have the same fear factor that so many other residents of DC are troubled by. A few inches of snow can shut down DC, freezing in place everything that dares to venture into the cold. Buses cannot even make it up the slight incline to Dupont Circle. Cars lose their traction on a light patina of snow, their drivers ill-equipped to negotiate the slippery roads. Visibility decreases in foggy snow, and ice builds up dangerously on most surfaces.

On January 19, 1982, my brother David was in town, serving an internship he needed for college. He had taken the day off to visit the Smithsonian, and so was not in the office suite as the snow fell throughout the day. The end of the day was fast approaching, and my thoughts had turned to how I would be getting home. I knew the metro would be slow and crowded, and that taxis would be slower than walking the two miles home. Suddenly, I heard on the radio that a plane had clipped the nearby 14th Street Bridge and sliced through the ice-covered Potomac and into the frigid water. Less than a mile from the site, the psychic call for help seemed immediate. As their physical bodies froze on contact, the passengers' spirits were stunned by the sudden turn of events. Rather than a trip to the warmth and sun of Florida, this apparently, for all but a few passengers, was the day of their transitioning. Moments later, another report came over that there had been a metro accident at the Smithsonian station. What would have been an immediate call to help the spirits of the passengers was tinged momentarily by concern for my brother's safety. This was before cell phones, so I knew it would be a while before I would know if he had been on the metro cars involved.

Once again, I turned my awareness toward the nearby river. I needed to get home to a quieter space to try to help. Somehow, I got home, though so distracted was I that I cannot remember if I took the metro, walked, or took a taxi. I remember distinctly entering my apartment and turning on the television.

As soon as I did and was able to confirm the horror of what I was seeing in my head, the connection with these spirits deepened, and I could feel myself under the water with them, could see them still strapped into their seats. I could see the physical people, but I also seemed to be communicating with their spirits that they could go forward and did not have to stay with their bodies. One couple still remains in my mind. I believe they were husband and wife, and both looked shocked physically and their spirits also wore the expression of shock. They seemed to leave together.

I started to question the validity of what I was seeing. It comes from being pragmatically skeptical about what I do. I am never sure, without some confirmation, that what I am sensing is absolutely true. That is why I like giving readings, because the information is verified immediately.

In the meantime, my thoughts returned to my brother, who finally arrived at my place, none the worse for wear. We had a great celebratory dinner of order-in lobsters (what decadence!) that night. I was very grateful that he was all right, but I was sorry that so many had lost their lives, apparently due to insufficient de-icing of the plane's wings.

The salvaging took place in the days that followed and not that evening. As they began to search for bodies, they had to bring up people still strapped in, or at least it seemed that way to me. There was the couple I had seen beneath the water; although they didn't as I recall actually show them, they described them in enough detail for me to recognize that they were indeed the couple that I had tried to help.

In the days that followed, as what I had seen beneath the water was confirmed, I was grateful to have been of help, but on the other hand, I hoped that I would never have to encounter such a disaster again and, for the most part, I have offered solace and guidance to smaller numbers of people who suddenly find themselves in the situation of sudden transition. It is a necessary form of reaching out and healing, but it also can be very emotionally trying, because the spirit(s) are often very confused and in great denial.

And then there was 9/11. The very last thing I remember before the entire world changed was that I was on the phone talking to my father. I had glanced at the television to see Sarah Ferguson being interviewed on Good Morning America. I turned away for a moment, and when I turned back, they were showing the World Trade Center with smoke pouring from the upper floors. At first I thought how dreadful that a small plane had hit the building, but in the ensuing minutes and hours, the horror of what was actually happening filtered across the airwaves. As the buildings crumbled, and the magnitude of the devastation became apparent, my first thought was how overwhelming this was, and my second thought, I am afraid to say, was to ask the larger interdependent web to not have to work this one, so to speak, to not have to wade into the physical and spiritual morass that had overtaken lower Manhattan. From my safe position in Rochester, I worried about my brother Martin, who worked in midtown, and his wife, who actually worked further downtown. It was much later that I found out that everyone I knew was safe, but my brother discovered he had lost over 20 friends in the devastation.

I had to drive into Rochester to teach a class that was amazingly not cancelled immediately by the administration. The minute I entered the building, the announcement came over the public address system that the building was being evacuated and everyone was told to leave downtown if at all possible, since they still not know the extent of the attack and whether smaller cities were also being targeted. I drove out of the parking garage and headed home. I passed the Rochester airport on the way, and the physical silence once all the planes were grounded was mitigated by the psychic sounds of distress. I arrived home as quickly as I could, knowing that I was being called to help. I knew I could not handle more than one person, and put that information "out there." Suddenly I found myself next to a woman named Anita who was wedged between two flat concrete slabs, along with what was left of her desk. She had dark, almost black curly hair and a bright yellow sweater. She was wavering between staying and leaving her body. It was evident that she was not going to make it, but I could sense this would be a relatively long process. I tried to calm her down, and told her to relax and that everything was going to be all right, which I knew it would be, once she had fully transitioned. She seemed comforted by my presence and I tried to stay with her as much as the circumstances of the day permitted.

My children got off their buses, papers in hand stating the schools had told them nothing of what was happening in order to allow parents to discuss it in their own way. It was a little later that I checked in on Anita, and she seemed to be still attached to her physical body, though I could tell that her transition was close. I became distracted and the next time I checked in, her spirit was no longer there. I said a quick prayer and sent best wishes along with her and turned to the larger tragedy as a spectator, rather than as a healer/helper.

The problem with being called to do such disaster work is the toll it can take on one's psyche. The physical devastation is horrific enough, but the attendant confusion and disorientation of those we are being called to help can have a harmful effect on even the best prepared psychic clairvoyant.

My friend Char also worked 9/11. She owns the New Age shop, Psychic's Thyme, in Rochester, and they held a rescue circle at the shop that day, and later, four people conducted a prayer circle. The rescue circle opened a portal to the other side through which the group became aware of events that had taken place on the plane and in the buildings. Char heard one little girl on one of the planes ask her mother, "Why are they (the terrorists) laughing?" The mother was crying. Another man said, "This isn't the airport." Char was pulled further into the portal. The others tried to psychically drag Char out, but she was being called to minister to those in need. She saw an Irish fireman (she could tell by the name on the nametag). She felt colder and colder and then she felt nothing. Then the fireman said, "We're almost out of the building." Apparently the fireman's spirit was trying to save Char. He didn't mean her harm. He had a hose over one shoulder as he was running up the stairs, and Char felt that he had transitioned on the staircase, but his spirit was still trying to do his duty. Char heard him say "mom" and then he dropped Char's hand.

After this arduous spirit healing/helping, it took 18 to 20 hours for Char to get totally back. Saltwater baths helped. (Salt is a great psychic cleanser, in addition to being used to ward off elemental energies.) As she continued to watch the news coverage, it became apparent that she had indeed been seeing people from the planes and from the buildings.

Apparently, one of the reasons that Char had become so thoroughly a part of the event was that another woman in the rescue circle had said "open the portal" and instead of looking through the door or window the psychic command would normally have created, Char had become the portal. In this state, Char had heard snippets of what they (the people in the buildings) were saying as they ran through her (as the portal) and into the white light. That day, Char had been wearing an amulet for opening psychic connection. Although she was well-trained in psychic rescue and healing work, this experience was frightening, even for her.

This incident points out, again, that if those with training in this sort of work can have such an arduous and frightening time of it, it is best that those with no knowledge whatsoever stay clear of this sort of endeavor. Which is not to say that "lay people" can't have a positive effect in time of disaster by offering prayer and gentle healing thoughts. Every bit of positive energy that flows towards the scene of an accident, no matter how big or small the event, will help to ease the pain of those who survive and ease the confusion of those whose time it is to transition. When learning of the passing of a solider in war, I try to send positive energy not only to the spirit of the soldier, but also to that person's family and loved ones, who also require comfort. When I hear of someone who has fallen ill, with anything from the common cold to cancer, I send love and healing energy (I think of it as psychic chicken soup). Since all illness is brought on by a disruption in energy flow, it is always my goal to try to help the person to regain balance in order to achieve a positive outcome.

Those involved in paranormal investigations also need to become versed in the ability to offer love and healing to those whose spirits may be stuck between the physical and spiritual realms. These earthbound spirits, as mentioned in Chapter 2, can become trapped here through traumatic death, reluctance to leave the space in which they spent time with a loved one, other emotional concerns, because of substance abuse, or because of their own misconception of death, brought on either by the religious beliefs they were taught, or ideas they developed on their own.

When paranormal investigators are called in to determine whether or not a location is indeed being "haunted," beyond proving or disproving the claim there is a responsibility to help alleviate the suffering of the discarnate spirit as well as the inconvenience and discomfort of the incarnate spirits who called the investigators in. While it is very important work to prove scientifically the presence of spirit in order to help persuade those reluctant or unwilling to acknowledge this plane of existence, and this field of work is highly commendable, it must always be kept in mind that the discarnate person is stuck for a reason and they have every right to move on to a healthier situation as does the homeowner, for example, to acquire a peaceful environment. Having a "haunted" environment is like having a house guest who has overstayed their visit and, even worse, the host may not even know the "guest."

Once it has been determined, either through instrumentation or psychically, that there is indeed an unwanted presence in a location, it is important to ascertain, if possible, who it is and why they have decided to stay there. Are they there for a reason or have they simply lost their way? Are they looking for someone specific or are they just comfortable where they are? In the case of a child, the spirit/ghost may be looking for a parent who actually transitioned decades or centuries earlier (ghosts are not necessarily of the current time period). Whether adult or child, trying to locate a family member on the other side to guide them is always helpful and can provide a calming influence during the process of weaning the spirit from the earth to spirit plane.

The one thing to remember is that this is most likely someone who is lost and has been so for a while and needs the energy of love and healing in order to make the transition complete. Sometimes, all it takes to encourage them to move on is to simply provide them with details of their current time and space. Perhaps they are somewhere they never were in a previous life (this can happen in the case of physical demise in an unfamiliar location, such as those who died in Air Florida 90). Or perhaps they are now in a time period far different from the last one during which they were incarnate. Pointing out the inconsistencies of their knowledge and experience with the space and time they are trying to inhabit now can provide all the information needed for them to realize that they need to move on.

In other situations, the spirit/ghost may have started the transition process in an altered state of consciousness, either from drug or alcohol use or from anesthetic or medication of one sort or another. In these cases, more time must be spent in explaining the situation they are in, reasoning with them, and pointing out their current physical state (or, actually, their lack thereof).

It is always helpful to call upon one's own guides to find spirits who know the trapped spirit. Having someone ready on the other side to guide the spirit to their new environment can be a welcome relief to all concerned.

In any case, encouraging the spirit/ghost to move toward the light (as cliché as it sounds) is the best way of getting them to open their eyes, so to speak, and realize there is something and someplace better than where they are. While this encouragement is taking place, it is most helpful to send love and healing energies to this person in order to ease their transition. Just as in the case of dealing with an incarnate spirit who is ill, this spirit/ghost is also in need of love and healing. Two or more investigators, joining their energies in this way can facilitate a peaceful and complete transition.

Paranormal investigators or anyone dealing with lost spirits should always try to release the spirit and encourage them to move to the next plane. Because we are inextricably bound to each other through the interdependent web, we actually have an obligation to do for others what we would want done for us.

In the same vein, when someone suffers a devastating loss, of a loved one or even of property, sending healing always helps to alleviate the pain. So, no matter how separated the person in need is from you, whether you know them or not, it is always best for them, and for you, to send a loving and healing wave of energy toward them.

Sometimes, the need for spiritual healing intervention can be much closer to home, and, rather than that intervention coming from an incarnate helper, the need may be answered by those in spirit.
It had been a long day of running errands and my children, Alex and Jane, at that time 12 and 9 respectively, were becoming understandably cranky following me from store to store.

"One more stop, and then, if you behave, I'll get you hot chocolate at Wegmans," I bribed them.

Suddenly, I had two perfect children and I was able to finish my last errand before the supermarket.

We stopped to get the hot chocolate first. The counter person asked Jane if she would like whipped cream on top and she said yes. Gingerly, she took the paper cup and tried to lick some of the whipped cream off. Immediately, the very hot drink spilled onto her shirt and soaked through to her stomach, which instantly turned bright red as blisters began to rise up.

I got some ice to put on the burn and her brother went to get the store manager, who came running to our aid. She saw Jane's stomach and immediately called the EMTs and two separate teams of them arrived. They examined her in the store office and agreed that she had sustained serious 1st degree burns. It looked pretty bad and they cautioned me that it would take about ten days to heal. They put a gauze bandage on the 4" x 5" burn to keep her clothes from irritating her skin. Through it all, Jane sat quietly, but obviously in considerable pain.

I called Jane's pediatrician from the store and the nurse called back immediately. I informed her of the EMTs' assessment. She agreed it would take at least 10 days to heal and told me what to buy so that I could tend to her during that time. She also wanted us to keep in touch with the office if there were any further developments.

When we finally got home, I gingerly took the bandage off, girding myself for the site of my poor daughter's injured skin. I stopped, the gauze pad falling to my lap . . . there was hardly any mark on Jane at all. In fact, there was only one very small, perhaps ¼" area that showed any trauma whatsoever, and it was just a little bit pinker than her normal skin color.

I was amazed and told Jane I thought it must be a miracle. That's when she told me that while I had been talking to the EMTs, she had been talking to Peepaw (the kids' nickname for my father who had transitioned that past July). She had asked him to help her, and apparently he had!

When the Wegman's claims person called the next day to see how Jane was doing, and I told her, she was also incredulous.

It is comforting to know that, even now, I can still count on Dad for help.

Healing can also be attained through meditation and by connecting with nature and remembering that we are part of a larger reality. Sitting quietly and stilling our mind to focus on one thing at a time can help to alleviate the stress of multi-tasking and multi-thinking we now all are engaged in. We are so busy all the time, that we never notice the moment that is passing by, what it feels like, how we feel in it. Instead, our minds are constantly whirling, like a hamster on a wheel, going quickly nowhere. This thought pattern can lead to many forms of mental and physical dis-ease. Learning to sit and still the mind can help gently break this mold imposed upon us by living in this ever-increasing hurry-up and over-stimulating world.

It can also be beneficial to practice visualization, which can help to bring about healing. Cancer patients have been known to visualize good cells destroying the cancerous cells, and have been much helped by this practice. Visualization is as easy as closing your eyes, imagining a peaceful scene, and taking calm, natural breaths. Especially in stressful situations, such as when in the dentist's chair or when having your blood pressure taken, visualization can help to keep you calm and focused on something more pleasant than pain or discomfort. And, when practiced while having your blood pressure taken, it can bring your numbers down significantly. The fact that you can do this, indicates that you can bring your blood pressure down at will, which will help to keep you healthier.

You can bring yourself into alignment with the cosmos and benefit from the calm and healing energies that are available to you. Here is an exercise I have been using and teaching for many years:

Sit with your back comfortably straight in your chair, feet flat on the floor and hands resting in your lap. Close your eyes and take a nice cleansing breath. Imagine that there is white energy flowing up from the earth and through your feet and into your body. Keep breathing slowly and deeply. The light is flowing up through your feet and around inside your body. It is warm and soothing. It is allowing you to be grounded to the earth.

Now, imagine that there is energy flowing down from high above you and into the top of your head. This energy, too, is a glowing white light that is refreshing and peaceful. This light is allowing you to feel in connection with the larger universe. Now, imagine and feel the light coming up from the earth and the light coming down from the sky mixing within you and allowing you to feel calm, refreshed, peaceful, and relaxed, as it fills your body with so much light that it actually begins to seem as though you are glowing this light into the space around you. Take as long as you wish to experience and enjoy this light moving within you and around you.

Now, sense that although the light is staying with you, it is no longer pouring down from above nor reaching towards you from below. As you continue to breathe peacefully, know that the light is now within you and is glowing from you and is there to keep you centered, at peace, relaxed, and stress-free. Anytime you feel you need or want to replenish this light energy, simply imagine the light coming up from the earth and down from the sky and filling you with that energy. Take a deep breath in, and release it slowly. When you are ready, open your eyes.

The benefits of this exercise are endless. Visualizing healing colors such as soothing greens and blues can utilize additional healing energies.

The act of healing, whether via ancient or modern methods, in person or at a very far distance, alone or in a group, and even incarnate or discarnate, helps to bond who we are, one to the other and to the larger seen and unseen world around us. It is almost as if disease exists to provide us with the opportunity to serve each other in peace and love.

Chapter 6

The Gift of Knowing:
Developing and Using Intuition

If the doors of perception were cleansed everything would appear to man as it is, infinite.
(William Blake)

Intuition is that psychic stock ticker that flows information through our daily lives. It is the prod that tells us to turn left or right to meet the person of our dreams, or to avoid danger. It is that still small voice, or that kick in the head or punch in the gut or that tickle in the brain that demands attention be paid to the minutiae that so often evades detection, but the importance of which can change our path down the street, or in life. Where does the information come from? It is constantly flowing over the interdependent web and is delivered to the recipient as a knowing or urging via conscious thought. Its closest cousin in the "clair" family would be claircognizance. Unlike clairvoyance or clairaudience or clairsentience, intuition most often presents itself in a way that causes (or tries to cause) a reaction or action in the recipient. Depending on the urgency or life-and-death level of the message, one can feel compelled to act NOW, or one can have a sense of knowing that seems to come from within one's being that was not there before.

Intuition and telepathy are two underutilized components of the human communication system. There are five physical senses available to humankind: sight, smell, taste, touch, hearing. Through these senses, all manner of sensory stimuli can be received and perceived. There are several non-physical senses available that allow extra-sensory perception of non-physical stimuli. These include: clairaudience (hearing), clairvoyance (sight), clairsentience (touching/feeling), clairalience (smell), and clairgustance (taste). In addition, there is claircognizance (knowing).

Intuition and telepathy are parts of the vast spectrum of human consciousness. Intuition is an internal knowing (that perhaps is in some way also informed by outside stimuli perceived via ESP), while telepathy permits communication through thought between people. Since we are inherently a part of the interdependent web, and thus all connected one to the other, telepathy is simple communication without spoken words. Intuition is knowing without external physical input.

How does one develop one's innate skill known as intuition? In some people, it is an ability that they are aware of and can utilize from their earliest days; in other people, it can develop over time, and for those seeking this ability to know, it can be developed by practice in listening to and trusting that other voice, that information that comes from within. For those now questioning the idea of hearing voices, let me assure you that this is nothing like those suffering from schizophrenia, which is more akin to actually hearing a full voice in one's head. It is somewhat different from hearing via clairaudience or while listening to those discarnate. It may be that intuition can more be likened to a non-voiced voice, by which I mean it is as though one is taking a cold medicine and when it starts to work, everything seems much clearer both physically in one's head and mentally. In a moment of intuitive insight, there is a sudden clear knowing.

This would be different from (though the result would be the same) when one's guardian spirit warns or encourages in a moment of need or want, but, of course, one would also need to develop the ability to trust that voice as well. There are a lot of voices, though none necessarily reflective of mental illness. I believe that some people who are in mental institutions because they are hearing voices may indeed be hearing voices, either guardians or discarnate beings, and while some may be of an unhealthy nature in the case of the latter, perhaps psychic counseling would help in those situations.

Just like anyone can develop their physical senses by using these and practicing with these, or learn to concentrate or think better using various techniques, one can learn to more regularly use one's intuition. For example, a classical musician needs to train his or her ear to hear music more acutely and accurately than someone who is not involved in that particular career. Someone who makes perfumes would need to train his or her nose to detect minute differences in fragrance. One can develop a more focused ability to concentrate and think by working the mind through a variety of developmental exercises that help to hone that skill.

Everyone is able to utilize their intuitive abilities, but not everyone desires to do so. In addition, as one learns to listen to that internal voice/impetus, one must at the same time learn to trust in it for guidance and information. One way to increase the effectiveness of this ability is to ask questions, e.g., should I turn left or right, watch this program or that (the one chosen may have pertinent information to a life question you are currently having), etc. Having asked the question and then acting on the impetus to act in a certain manner that comes in answer to that question will help you to learn to pay attention to the decision and where it seems to come from and then note the outcome.

To increase your trust in your intuition, write down the questions and answers as these arise, and the results of acting on that information. Keeping a journal is a perfect way to keep all of your experiences together in one place. By journaling, you have a record of hard evidence of your progress. Relying solely on your memory is hazardous since the human mind likes to fill in the gaps and you may come to not trust your memory of specific instances, if indeed you remember these at all.

Keeping a journal as a record of your experiences with intuition or interactions with spirit or other events of a paranormal nature will help to reinforce the truth of what you are experiencing and give you solid evidence that these events and instances are indeed occurring. When you want to try your hand at communicating with spirit, or developing a relationship with your spirit guide, a journal is indispensable. Write the questions you have for the discarnate being (people and guides only please . . . no trying to communicate with negative energies) down in your journal and wait a moment to allow the spirit to respond. Write down what you perceive as the person's answer. At first, this may seem as though you are simply making up the written conversation, but as time goes on and you practice more regularly, you will find the answers becoming more pertinent and useful. Also as time goes on, you may find yourself experiencing other phenomenon that you really should record as soon as possible so you can learn from these and trust in their validity. Purchasing some inexpensive composition notebooks would be a good idea right about now if you truly want to grow as an incarnate spirit.

It is helpful, especially when you are starting out trying to communicate with your own intuition or with spirits, to eke out some quiet moments in which to do so. It is helpful to make sure you have pen and journal ready and then close your eyes and concentrate on your breathing for a minute or two. Then, when you are feeling peaceful and able to concentrate, write down the question you would like to ask or a statement you would like a response to. It could be as simple as "what is the name of my guardian spirit?" You could also ask who will be the next person to call you, or what will be the lead story on the news. As soon as you finish writing down your question, stop and, for a better direction, listen for an answer. You may hear words, but you may also feel compelled to write down an answer that seems to be coming from nowhere in particular. Sometimes the answers will make perfect sense or correctly provide information, and sometimes they won't. Either way, keeping a record will help you to recognize the moments when the information turns out to be correct and what that feels like or sounds like, and then you will begin to trust in that information and its method of delivery. Soon, you will begin to recognize when your intuitive self, or when external spirit, is communicating with you, and you will begin to trust the information.

Trusting intuition can be a daunting task, often requiring courage, and not a little bit of accepting inklings and information that on the surface can seem to make little sense, but will, in fact, lead to the one piece of the puzzle that has been missing, or the letter tile that will complete the word, or the step that will change your life or lead to world peace—you never really know!

While working on this chapter a friend of mine mentioned that if her boyfriend had not listened to that guiding voice at the exact right moment and swept her into a passionate kiss at the very beginning of their relationship, there might not have been a further relationship to enjoy. While it may have been an impulse of a more mundane nature, according to the gentleman, it was more than that; it was an intuition that, albeit early in their meeting, this was the moment for action. He (or she) who hesitates is lost, or alone, or left wanting, or on the wrong road. Sometimes it is the feeling that one must look up and then finding oneself gazing into the eyes of a future (or far past . . . as in past-life) lover.

Of course, there is the need to be receptive to the information presenting itself. Here you may be sensing that it is sometimes difficult to differentiate when information is being given to you via intuition or spirit guidance and, indeed, it can be hard to tell the difference. Often it does not matter—what matters is the validity of that information and the impact that information will have on your life.

The shift in conscious awareness is a subtle one and sometimes it is hard to recognize it has taken place. We all have access to the information available through utilizing intuition and becoming cognizant of input from discarnate spirit (via clairvoyance, etc.) as well as other incarnate people (via telepathy). This helps to exemplify the reality of the interdependent web as the foundation for our collective being. We are, indeed, a microcosm held within a macrocosmic universe. This recognition will help us to evolve into the compassionate, interrelated beings, the one family, we are meant to be.

Intuitive insights can occur at any time, in any circumstance. Whether we pay attention to these or not is a matter of our own freewill. Even though I have had many, many intuitive moments, sometimes even I ignore the information so freely being handed to me, and other times I find it impossible to ignore the gentle prodding that is pushing me in a particular direction or giving me pertinent information.

When I was in high school, I belonged to a girls' singing group that sang around town. One day, towards the end of the school year, we were singing at a local elementary school. Normally, we would stop on the way back to high school for a milk shake or soda. This day, I felt that I absolutely had to get back to the school. I was adamant about it, in fact. The other girls went out for the soda and one of the drivers took me back to the school. The moment I arrived at my locker, my father appeared to tell me that my mother's mother had died. My intuition had told me I needed to be at a certain place at a certain time, and the impulse was so strong, I could not ignore it. While going for the soda would not have changed the outcome, being there when my dad needed to find me was important for him, and for me.

When I first arrived at Fredonia as an underage freshman, I became friends with another 17-year old who also could not get into the town's drinking establishments (the drinking age at the time was 18). Jeffrey and I took advantage of a lot of the events on campus. One night, we walked over to the union to see a movie. On the way over, Jeffrey was bemoaning the fact that he had lost his wallet. Without stopping to think of what I was saying, and at the same time feeling compelled to say it, I asked him why he needed his wallet back so badly. He replied he needed his ID card, and I told him, again because I was compelled to do so, that that didn't seem like a very good reason. He offered that his driver's license was in there, and I told him he could get a new one. Finally, he said there were pictures that he particularly liked of his family. As soon as he said that, I told him he would get the wallet back within 15 minutes, and of course, new friends that we were, he looked at me as though I was insane (I have since recognized that look as an occupational hazard). I said nothing more about the wallet as we took our place in line to get our tickets. Suddenly Jeffrey, who was allergic to quite a number of things, realized he had forgotten to bring tissues with him. I told him to run back to the dorm and get some and I would get the tickets and our seats. Within 15 minutes, he came back, tissue box in one hand and wallet in the other. He seemed in a state of shock. I asked what had happened. It turned out that the minute he entered his dorm, a girl who had been standing at the office window turned towards him and gasped, asking if he had lost his wallet, which she was holding in her hand. She had recognized him from the ID card.

Jeff tucked the wallet into his pocket, tissues clutched in his hand, and just kept staring at me, and opening and closing his mouth like a fish, unable to quite articulate whatever he wanted to say. All he could get out was, "how did you . . ." What he didn't know is that at that point I didn't know how I had known what I had known.

What I do realize is that each step, each pebble on the path being trod upon, can produce the link to the next and to the next in an almost seamless flow that is one's life, even though often we do not recognize this. Being aware of this flow, greased as it can be by being receptive to intuition, can cause each footstep to be placed with surety and confidence that life is unfolding as it was meant to. I like to think that the way made easy is the path we are supposed to be on and although moment to moment one <u>can</u> perceive each step as arduous, fraught with danger, and perhaps painful, developing an awareness that this is an unfoldment can help to alleviate stress and indeed ease one's journey.

On the other hand, ignoring this can cause frustration, inconvenience, and a sense of discomfort similar to wearing your right shoe on your left foot—something is not quite right.

Once, I was provided with intuitive insight, and didn't recognize it, thus causing myself a certain amount of inconvenience. On a particular summer's day, I was scheduled to work at Psychic's Thyme where I give readings. As I prepared to go to work, I thought of going to a large, nearby big box store. I knew I had no reason to go there and needed nothing sold there and so dismissed the idea. A little while later, a co-worker from Psychic's Thyme called and asked if I could give her a ride in to the store and if could meet her at the very big box store I had been thinking of earlier. I agreed to pick her up there. As I pulled out of my driveway, I got the distinct impression that rather than take the expressway, I should take secondary roads. I ignored the information and got onto the expressway. Almost immediately I found that there was a detour that led me miles in the opposite direction of my intended destination. The ensuing back-up of cars trying to negotiate the detour delayed my picking up my friend by more than 20 minutes. The moral of the story is that when the information is that specific and insistent, one should strive to listen to and heed it.

Sometimes we get information and even if we believe it, there is nothing that we can do to change the outcome. The assassinations of both Abraham Lincoln and John F. Kennedy were foreseen by their respective secretaries, who warned the former not to go to the theatre and the latter not to go to Dallas. Obviously, neither man listened to the intuition of their secretaries and the outcome in both cases changed the nation.

Three days before her assassination, I awoke believing that Benazir Bhutto had been killed in Pakistan. I fully expected to see the reports of her death as I went to turn on the television. I was quite surprised to see that nothing of the sort had happened. On December 27, 2007, I awoke to the news that she had, indeed, been assassinated. There is nothing I could have done to stop this event, so, as I have in past similar instances, I wonder what knowing ahead of time means, what the purpose is. Does it indicate/testify only that there is a larger web of information and communication available, which my intuition tapped into? Does this pre-perception, pre-cognition of these larger events, these widely verifiable events give more solid proof to the existence and availability of this information? This is a question that I still have not found a satisfactory answer to.

Sometimes, our intuition tries to guide us on a path we selected before our birth as a part of a general plan for this lifetime. But, often, a person who decides to go in a particular direction, may not be doing so in response to an inner impulse to do so, but rather because of peer pressure, or peer involvement, or defiance, or any number of reasons that, while not ringing quite right, seems to be the best way to go. It is almost as though rather than hearing the clear, dulcet tones of intuition (or our guides), we are fixated on the incessant drone of that imp of perversity that can so often and easily lead us astray. Knowing and acknowledging the difference is often not learned until later in life, if at all.

When I was in high school, there were many areas I was interested in, but a majority of my friends had some involvement in music. We belonged to chorus, and choir, and the small girls' singing group I mentioned earlier. We were in band, and jazz band, and orchestra. Being a part of a creative group is a wonderful outlet at any age, but in high school, it provides a nice, safe haven where one can fit in and belong and still be different, as was my case. I loved singing, but unfortunately my instrument was truly one of the more solo ones . . . I was a pianist, and though I derived little pleasure from it, I was quite good, and so I found myself auditioning for SUNY Fredonia on this instrument I had nick-named "88 ways to make a mistake."

I knew I didn't want to perform on the piano, because the few times I had, I hated the experience, applause not-with-standing, so I decided the best course was to major in theory and conducting, both of which I enjoyed, though I could never clearly see myself making a living doing either. Unfortunately, I was accepted, and so began my college career as what was known at Fredonia as a zippie, because no one ever actually saw a music major, just a faint body zipping around from class to class, practice room to rehearsal hall. Every part of my being knew that I was in the wrong major, but I had prepared so strenuously for the audition, I wasn't sure how to extricate myself from what was obviously one of my poorest choices. I knew I should be in English, where I could read and write to my heart's content, but I could not figure out how to finally leave that black-and-white monster behind and move back to a path I had known was there for years, but which I had ignored, because neither reading nor writing were social activities, and music and musical theater were (except for that instrument of torture I was chained to, the piano).

As the semester progressed, the social activities seemed to overtake my practice and theory time (the later in great measure involved training my ears to hear music precisely as preparation for conducting). As I approached my first semester juries (when musicians must play or sing before a panel of teachers who would then issue a grade), I knew I wasn't ready and then I became horribly ill. I vaguely remember sitting down at the piano to play, a 104-degree temperature making my eyes perceive the keyboard as swimming black and white tongues that I was trying to catch. Somehow I got a C for the semester in piano. Unfortunately, by the time I got home, was taken to a doctor, and diagnosed with bronchitis and tonsillitis, the fever had destroyed the top portion of hearing in my right ear. Without that ability to hear those notes, any possibility of pursuing a career in theory went out the window and since I didn't want to play the piano for a living, my music career, so-to-speak, came, thankfully, to an end. By the time I was a few weeks into the next semester, I had realized the hearing loss and I was tired of struggling.

I have often wondered if, had I followed what my intuition had been trying to guide me to do, rather than defiantly going in what turned out to be the wrong direction, I would have made different choices, different selections. But, then, I would not be where I am now, so I know I had to take those missteps to get to this point. Did my intuition lead me far enough in that direction to ensure this result? Is there another outcome that would have allowed me to gain the same insights? I don't know. What I do know is that I was well fore-warned that music, at least at that point in my life, was not what I was going to end up doing.

Since then, I have been lucky enough to go back to music as a hobby and along the way discovered that I had a reasonably good singing voice, but the events of that first year of college taught me that all things happen in their own time, and whether that coincides with my own ideas of what should be happening at a certain moment, or the universe's, or some parallel part of me, I don't know. I do know if I had listened to that still small voice slightly earlier, and switched majors, I probably would still have all my hearing.

One can also find the solution to problems or challenges through putting a question out into the universe, confident that the answer will indeed be supplied. Of course, one must listen for the answer. In writing this chapter, I found myself stumped at one point of how to communicate a rather (I thought) intricate idea. I searched through many books, trying to get a handle on how best to describe a concept, but nowhere did I find exactly the answer I was looking for. Instead, the answer came in an e-mail from an editor of a small newspaper I wrote for.

I shared the progression of events with my brother David, to whom I sent this e-mail:

> I wrote several pages yesterday in chapter 6 (Intuition). I knew I was having problems describing exactly what I mean by intuition. This morning, I received an e-mail from Dan (my editor) regarding a story idea about a man who is involved with a business model based on intuitive insight which appears to be a problem-solving-specific implementation of noetics, which basically deals with "intuitive ways of knowing" (FYI: The Institute for Noetic Sciences was started by Astronaut/Physicist Edgar Mitchell).

So I started by looking up the expert Dan is pitching to me and then it reminded me of Mitchell's Noetics. Visiting that site helped me to realize a better way of approaching my discussion of intuition, i.e., that more than being an "out there" thing, it is an "in here" thing, that intuition is simply a different level of consciousness that is available to everyone, yet widely under-utilized.

Then, I realized that this serendipitous discovery path was indeed a prime example of synchronistic events (which is part of Chapter 7) appearing when needed, so this (above) will be a great transition from Chapter 6 to Chapter 7.

We are all connected, the information flowing over the web (interdependent, not internet) is there for us to access and from which we can gain knowledge and insight.

An interesting side story to this is that the gentleman I interviewed for the article and I seemed to have a great deal in common and a telephone romance ensued for a very brief period of time—days, not even weeks—because my intuition started whispering and then screaming that this was not something I should be pursuing and I extricated myself as quickly (and gently) as possible.

The psychic waves that constitute the transmission and reception of intuition, telepathy, and other modes of paranormal reception and perception of knowledge are like radio waves . . . even when the radio is turned off, the waves are still there. Turn on and tune in the radio, and the waves are perceived as voices or music. In paranormal reception, you are the receiver, and with practice you will tune in and trust that knowledge and information being beamed toward you.

There are, essentially three sources from whence these informative waves of energy originate: in the subconscious, as a pool of resources available to you from the vast sea of experiential data you have collected throughout your life; in the connection between telepathy—the sending and receiving of information—and intuition from external sources; and in the superconscious, which is contained in the interdependent, cosmic web of the universe.

By practicing being receptive to the energy waves of intuition and telepathy and learning to trust in those waves, the frequency of intuitive and telepathic moments will naturally increase. This increase in trusting self and the information being presented will help to increase your awareness of and interaction with others, both in- and discarnate, bound as we are, in the interdependent web.

Chapter 7

The Gift of Miracles:
It's Not Just a Coincidence

*Somewhere, something incredible
is waiting to be known.
(Blaise Pascal)*

While starting to work on this chapter, it happened that I was listening to the television and reading at the same time. I do this a lot and once in a while it so happens that as I am reading, someone on the television will say the words I am reading at that precise moment. The confluence of the words always seems to have some meaning for the moment or the day. Nothing earth-shattering, surely, but a few overlapping words of guidance or inspiration.

At that particular moment, on that particular day this week, the words were "brought together." This instance of synchronicity seems to have had a deeper meaning than usual, for synchronicity, which the moment demonstrated so well, brings together moments in time, places in space, and people in all manner of time and space realities. All of these are normally spread out over the interdependent web until brought together by the synergistic quality of synchronicity. Why bring in synergy at the same time? It would appear that the two actualizing energies can be intertwined at that "a-ha!" moment.

Synchronous events are not simply coincidences, because the resulting recognition of the synchronicity always imparts a deeper meaning or reaction to the overlay. This then, is where synergy comes in, because at that moment of synchronous recognition, the parts merge to become a greater whole.

When a synchronous moment occurs, it is an event designed to catch and direct our attention to something larger than a mundane recognition of individual parts. To return to the "brought together" synchronistic moment of two days ago, it refocused the need for me to once again raise the idea that it isn't merely hearing voices or seeing people from the other side that this book is about, but rather the idea that the ability to do so, points to the larger reality of which we are a part. This can serve to expand our incarnate experience by increasing our awareness of the interconnectedness of everything and everyone.

While there are many recorded instances of miracles/coincidences/synchronistic moments occurring throughout history, it is not the major ones that I am addressing here, but rather the ones that occur every day to each of us. Is it a miracle or coincidence when we need a parking space in a certain location and at the precise moment that we are nearing that location, a space opens up? In a raging downpour, I would be hard pressed to not recognize this as a miracle. When I am thinking of a friend from whom I have not heard in a while, and the phone rings and it is that friend, is that a miracle? Since there are truly no coincidences, why, yes it is.

Why are there no coincidences to be found? Because the universe runs far more logically than the randomness of a coincidence would require. While we have freewill, the non-physical forces that act on and through the interdependent web also have the freewill to interact with this plane and work to gain our attention, or interject their influence on this plane. Synchronistic moments and miracles occur to reaffirm to us the idea that there is something larger than us working in the same space/time in which we find ourselves.

A hungry person who is short on money and then suddenly finds laying on the ground a $5 bill is immediately (one would hope) drawn into a questioning mode, or at least cognizant of his or her good fortune. Someone or something has caused that $5 bill to be exactly where that hungry person could find it.

For most people, it is easier to call answering the phone to find the person they were just that moment thinking about a coincidence, which relegates it to the realm of the mundane and unimportant, than to step back and recognize the miracle that has just occurred.

On Friday, November 30, 2007, my daughter sang a solo in her school's talent show. She did an excellent job, as expected, and we drove home pleased with her performance. As we pulled into our driveway, we gasped . . . the darkness sensitive security light above the garage was shining brightly. Why was this an amazing event? Because exactly a year before, on the night of the talent show at which my daughter also sang, as we prepared to leave for the school, my garage door ceased to work, as did this light. The light never went on again until this night. As sure as the light poured into the darkness, illuminating the cold night, I was sure that the light would not come on again the following evening, nor thereafter . . . and it hasn't. I had the definite feeling that it was a sign of congratulations to my daughter from another time/space being abutting our own. I honestly believed it was my dad, saying, "good job, Jane . . . way to go pal."

I classify this as a synchronistic/miraculous event because the timing was not haphazard, but rather directly related to an event that had just occurred. If the light had gone on, say, the Wednesday following the talent show, I would have thought perhaps it was a nice moment to have the light go on, but it would not have been of the synchronous nature that it was on the night of the talent show. Then, it was up to us to recognize that yes, indeed, some information or thought was being communicated to us, in the only way possible and reasonable, at that moment. It was not, for example, that a bit of siding had broken loose, or a tree branch fallen, or an unexpected refund arrived in the mail. It exactly related to the event that had occurred the year previous. Talent show night. 364 other days for the light to have gone on, and yet it was on this night it shined brightly. While it would be more of an irritation than anything else, the breaking of the garage door and the light the previous year could have also been a sign, but it would not have been recognizable as such. On the other hand, it is possible that the occurrence on the night of the first talent show was, in fact, a set up for the event of the second talent show night. The first event had to have happened for the second event to impart meaning.

Dad's ability to communicate from his new environs was quite prevalent during the year following his transition, and his main mode of interacting, it seemed, was through creating moments of synchronicity, those "aha" moments that would grab my attention more than anything else.

On July 7, 2004, two days after dad transitioned, all the family had gathered in Rochester for the funeral the following day. I was not sure where the cemetery was, and so Alex, Jane, and my cousin Barb, drove over after dinner to make sure we would not get lost in the morning. I found the cemetery easily, and made a u-turn to get back out to the main road. As I did so, the car suddenly filled with the distinctive odor of dad's room at the nursing home. It was unmistakable, and was smelled by everyone in the car. As we pulled out of the cemetery, the odor began to dissipate, and disappear. The concurrent acts of being at the cemetery and detecting that particular odor qualified as a synchronous moment . . . one thing did not cause the other to happen, and yet there was a definite interrelatedness to these two events. In addition, it is interesting to note that the odor did not occur anywhere else at any other time, but only as we were leaving the cemetery.

A little over two months after my father transitioned, I had been thinking of him and the upcoming Fiddler's Fair at the Genesee Country Village, a living museum that presents the architecture and routine of daily life in this part of New York State a hundred or more years ago. We had gone together to this event on a couple of occasions. The last one, two years previous, ended with Dad needing to be transported in a golf cart back to the main entrance because he could not breathe.

As I parked in my driveway, I started sobbing because I was missing the physical being that dad was. I had a local radio station playing and someone was interviewing a musician. Over my sobs, I heard the musician say, "Yes, that's when I ran into Phil." Hearing my dad's name at that moment, I stopped crying and focused on what was being said. A few lines later, the man said, "It was quite a coincidence." Then the interviewer said, "It seems dreams really do come true." I saw this clearly as one of those coincidences sent to calm or elucidate. I was immediately filled with a deep feeling of peace.

Of course, this was not the first time that I had experienced synchronicity in relation to my dad. From the time he was in the process of transitioning, and continuing for several months, yellow roses would appear at appropriate moments on a rose bush I did not previously even know was in my garden. Now, it is important to note that on the day I was born, my dad sent me yellow tea roses so he would be the first man to send me flowers. The yellow rose became a special flower between the two of us.

The first flower appeared the day of his funeral 7/8. Suddenly, where there had been no yellow rose bush before, there appeared a yellow rose. Then on 9/22, the day of Autumnal Equinox, there was another small rose not fully unfolded, but obviously there and it surely was there the day before, which was his sister Blanche's birthday. On 9/29 I noted that the rose was still blooming while a white one that had bloomed in the week past was quite spent, the petals already fallen.

On 7/24/05, I noted that "For the past week or so, there have been four small buds on the yellow rose bush. These seemed too small to produce the full size roses of last year. In the past few days two of the buds opened, not full size, but larger than tea roses. Sometime between yesterday and today, the other two roses bloomed."

I discovered that these blooms coincided with my dad's yerzeit, a day commemorating the transition of a loved one occurring exactly one year according to the Jewish calendar after their passing. Again, the roses had appeared in a timely manner!

But, the moments of miraculous synchronicity were not limited to roses. On the Saturday following his funeral, my children had gone to visit their dad, and I was not in the mood to sit idly alone at home. I walked down the street to a barn sale that was being held. I had been to this barn before as the gentleman who owns it periodically opens its doors to the public in order to sell the antiques and just plain old things contained therein. I was drawn to a pile of sheet music and was amazed to find several songs that had been among dad's favorites, including "Glory of Love." As I flipped the pages, I could almost hear my dad singing. I was at first reluctant to attach any deep meaning or import to these finds.

Then, as I dug deeper in the pile, I suddenly came upon a Cornell Composition Book that had never been used. Now, that qualified as a synchronistic moment, a miracle if you will, because that is where my dad did his work for his doctorate degree. There are dozens of colleges it could have been from, but it was from the one college I most associated with dad. Plus, while he was studying there, yours truly was born, and so the meaning of making this find became more solidified for me as one of intention and not just a random occurrence. There is no doubt in my mind that dad was trying to communicate with me.

Discarnate spirits often utilize the attention grabbing over the subtle in order to communicate their continued involvement in the incarnate spirit's life. The fact that it had not been written in I took as a sign that perhaps I was to focus on my writing, rather than avoiding it. My dad was very eager for me to make it as a writer, especially since he knew it meant so such to me to do so.

Still, I needed more confirmation of the "specialness" of the composition book, so I called Cornell on Monday and found someone who was familiar with the history of the bookstore and what had been sold there over the years. I described the cover of the book, and the person was fairly sure that it would have been sold during the period when my dad attended the school and I was born. Coincidence? I think not!

Synchronistic events often occur when a discarnate spirit is trying to get our attention, as well as when the larger energies and entities of the interdependent web are trying to do so. When we become aware of the event and then acknowledge the larger impact of this communication, we become awakened to the role we play in the scheme of the universe. It is as though those of a vibrational plane other than this one are trying to invite us to a party we are not aware of. Indeed, it is their way of welcoming us as like beings, because, as essentially spirit, we are the same, no matter the level of vibration we are existing on at this particular moment.

Acknowledging being a part of this larger reality, the true substance of which is what everyone is, whether living down the street, on the other side of the world, or on another plane, has the power to change our perspective of what constitutes reality and what constitutes our relationship with others. If everyone on this plane, knowingly or not, is receiving these moments of synchronicity, and if the main idea, the overriding import of this, is that we are all one in the interdependent web, then our perspective of the others in this plane would need to change.

The journal I encouraged you to start keeping earlier is a handy place in which to keep a record of the synchronistic moments that occur in your life. The more you record your synchronistic moments, the more of these moments you will seem to have. Since these events are always happening, if you take the time to write these down when these occur, it will impress you with the frequency with which they actually do occur, and you will realize that these have been happening all along. In essence, keeping the journal will help you to expand and accept your new awareness of the real reality rather than the one you previously thought was real. In essence, you will begin to expect these miracles, and will begin to see signs and symbols springing up in unexpected places and in unexpected ways.

There is a difference between synchronistic events and miracles. The former have no <u>apparent</u> causal agent creating the simultaneous occurrence of the event. A miracle, on the other hand seems to require an action or cause. If one receives a miraculous healing at Lourdes, then the person has traveled to the shrine, has been prayed for or had a drink of the water, or bathed in it. Any of these actions invite the healing into the person's life. While it is a miracle, it is not synchronistic . . . a cause can be noted. In addition, if someone is healed because someone or a circle of people prayed for that event, again, it is not acausal, but rather caused by the intervention of the prayer(s). It could still be a miracle, because the act of praying is inviting an intervention in the course of normal events by a (for lack of a better word) supernatural force. If there is an awareness that one is, in effect, asking for a miracle, and thereby helping to facilitate that miracle, then the idea of independent, acausal events is missing in order to claim it as synchronous. For example, several years ago I was shoveling my driveway after a heavy snow. I was feeling a little defeated because I had shoveled the driveway several times previously on that particular day. I stopped for a moment and asked anyone listening on another plane to send me some help. Within a few minutes a couple of acquaintances happened by with a snowplow and in minutes my driveway was clear. Was this synchronistic? No—I had asked for help and then received it. My asking caused the universe to hear my request and then kindly fulfill it. Was it a miracle? Yes—the event occurred out of the "natural" order of things, and while I hoped for help, I did not know I was going to receive it.

Synchronistic events can be seen as miracles, but in reality synchronicity requires that the simultaneous occurrence of events be acausal, and asking, consciously or not, for a miracle and receiving it would be causal. Receiving from positive thinking (another mode of prayer) would also be causal, not acausal.

Miracles can also occur unbidden. Just today I heard of an 11-month old baby who had miraculously survived after a tornado carried him 300 feet from his home. He was found in the same field as his transitioned 24-year old mother. It is as though a hand was reached across the interdependent web to carry the child to safety. Then, one must ask, why not the mother? His survival was an unbidden miracle, but his mother's passing may also be a part of some plan not yet (obviously) understood. It may be that, despite appearances, her mission had been fulfilled and she was ready to carry on on the next plane.

My dad was a ball-turret gunner in World War II. His plane was to bomb bridges in Germany. Unfortunately, the German government had instructed people to go hide under the bridges in order to be safe from the bombings. One day, as his plane was bombing a bridge in Rosenheim, Germany, the bomb missed its target and the people under the bridge survived. Years later, my father, then a professor at State University of New York at Brockport met a man at a faculty party. The man, speaking with a German accent, and my dad were talking about the war. The man recounted a day when he was seeking shelter under a bridge in Rosenheim as the bombers came overhead. He said he was very lucky, because the bomb completely missed the bridge. As they talked further, trying to pinpoint when this happened, it became apparent that it was my dad's plane that had dropped the bomb that had missed the bridge, thus inadvertently saving the life of the German man. "It was a good thing you had bad aim," the man said to my dad.

The bad aim actually qualifies as a miracle. The bombs had hit other bridges on other days, but for the reason of saving this man (and those around him), this bomb had missed. It is not a stretch to believe those under the bridge would pray to be spared. The occurrence of their later meeting would qualify as a synchronistic one. Neither knew the other prior to meeting at the party. Acausal circumstances brought them together.

Now, sometimes moments of synchronicity or even miracles are delivered via what we might call angels or helpers. We are surrounded by angels. Although we don't see their wings, they are everywhere. There is the smiling angel who says good morning on the way to work. There are angels who hold the door for a mother with two small children and a heavy grocery bag. There is the angel who listens when no one else will; maybe that angel simply allowed someone to share a moment, and just maybe that angel saved a life. Then there might be an angel who shows up at an accident just in time to pull a survivor from burning wreckage. We never know which angels are of this plane and which are visiting, momentarily, from elsewhere.

I had had a very difficult day. Details are unimportant, and best forgotten. The lost details delivered me to the moment of angelic blessings. I suddenly had a need for Paul McCartney's new CD, *Memory Almost Full*. Only Starbucks was carrying it, so I headed there. As I entered, I must have looked like I felt . . . exhausted, a little defeated, frustrated . . . the woman behind the counter welcomed me in a lilting Jamaican accent that warmed my soul. I picked the CD from the rack at the counter and asked for a latte. She said, "Don't worry I'll make you a special latte." With that, she turned and worked her beverage-mixing magic. I paid and she handed it to me, saying something about now I would feel better, now this was just for me. Thanking her, I turned and walked from the store.

I looked at the cup . . . this is what it said: "In reality, hell is not such an intention of God as it is an invention of man. God is love and people are precious. Authentic truth is not so much taught or learned as it is remembered. Somewhere in your pre-incarnate consciousness you were loved absolutely because you were. Loved absolutely, and in reality, you still are! Remember who you are!" (Bishop Carlton Pearson, author, speaker, spiritual leader and recording artist)

I was amazed at the obvious selection of this cup, and went back inside to thank the woman for this uplifting message. She shook her head and said it was just the next one in the stack . . . it was a needed miracle and the woman, Debra, was my Starbucks Angel.

Now, you see, we must become the angels. The angel who smiles and says good morning, the angel who touches someone who has not been touched in a very long time. Maybe even the angel who helps in the crisis. We each and every one of us must become angels.

A lot of moments of synchronicity and/or miracles seem to occur when we are less than whole physically, mentally, or spiritually. While sometimes moments of synchronicity just seem to happen whatever state we are in, these are just as likely to occur when we are in need of an answer, or some information, or help, or guidance.

One day, I was running early in the morning, and while doing so, I was wondering if I really am a writer and if it would ever be possible to make a living writing, or if my writing had any chance of having an impact on anyone, as I hoped it would. I kept on running, but I asked for a sign to encourage me to continue on that path (writing, not running). Down from a clear blue, early morning sky, with not a bird in sight, a single small feather wafted down in front of me and landed. Since I have always associated feathers with writing (quills, etc.), and also as a symbol of freedom and hope, I didn't hesitate a moment in recognizing this as a miracle. I had asked for guidance, and (rather immediately) received it. Proof that I have yet to give up are the words I type here.

Both synchronicity and miracles affirm the existence of something outside of our limited perception of reality acting upon that reality. What then can we learn from synchronous moments and miracles? Is there a lesson to be learned? Is there a message of comfort or information to be received? The larger lesson to be learned, beyond whatever is immediately gained by the occurrence, is that there is something larger interacting with us and often guiding us in our daily lives. Whether physical angels being acted upon to serve a purpose for another or a larger group, or spirit angels, who reach across time and space to intervene, or higher beings trying to impart a message or ensure a course of action, "there are more things in heaven and earth . . .than are dreamt of in your philosophy" as Hamlet said to Horatio. It is hard to find a quote that better serves to illustrate the limitations we set upon ourselves on this plane by not allowing that there might, indeed, be something more, something beyond our very limited philosophies. Synchronicity and miracles help us to redirect our focus and contemplate, if only for a few moments, something or a presence, also acting in this limited here and now who might not necessarily be limited to this space and time.

And, this being so, as proved by the occurrence of the events discussed in this chapter and surely experienced by you, the reader who has been drawn here at this moment, does this not widen, even incrementally, our perception, and lead us to question if what we perceive as a narrow reality is not actually much, much larger and much more complex than we can imagine? And, if some of us are unknowing catalysts for the miraculous and synchronistic, doesn't this point to a deeper interconnectedness between us? For if we, physically encased spiritual beings, are acted upon by angels in discarnate spirit form to be angels in incarnate spirit form, isn't there a wider truth of our interconnectedness within the physical and non-physical elements of the interdependent web? And, if we are so connected, then isn't it time we started relating to each other on a deeper, more spirit-aware level?

As I prepared to begin editing Chapter 8 and 7, (for reasons I don't fully understand, I started my first edit of this book with Chapter 10, and worked backwards), I looked at the title of Chapter 7 (The Gift of Miracles: It's Not Just a Coincidence) and suddenly felt compelled to Google my dad's widow. Now, this woman had exhibited much unkindness and cruelty in the days after my father transitioned, and I could think of no good reason to uncover any information about her. ("Coincidentally" the company she works for is one floor below mine and I have the knowledge that for five hours a day she is too near to me physically. I block her vibration from floating upwards.)

Anyway, I Googled her and discovered *her* father had transitioned less than two weeks previously. This was a shock (I thought he had passed several years prior) and the "coincidence" that I would check into her life at this pivotal moment seemed to have occurred at the urging of someone (dad?) outside of my physical environs.

But wait, there's more . . . I picked up my son and told him of the day's events. He thought that it was odd, especially since, he told me, he had seen someone on TV that morning who resembled her and had, for the first time in a long time, been thinking of her that day. A coincidence? Hardly . . .

Like a tapestry, or a web, all things are interconnected in the universe. Because of this, at any moment in time you are connected to any other moment in time, any other space, and any other person. Because of this infinite number of connections, there are no coincidences. All is purposely interwoven into the fabric of the interdependent web.

Chapter 8

The Gift of Empathy:
Caring Enough to Receive

*It is only with the heart that one can see rightly.
What is essential is invisible to the eye.
(Antoine de Saint-Exupéry)*

Empathy is the ability to perceive the physical, mental, and emotional state of another, to offer understanding, comfort, and healing, with or without the recipient's conscious awareness.

Empathy is similar to sympathy in that there is an awareness of the distress of another, but while sympathy can foster compassion, empathy goes one step beyond, and the actual sensation of the person experiencing the discomfort enters the perception of the empathizer as a tangible feeling of a mental, emotional, and/or physical nature. You actually feel another person's pain or distress. In addition, empathy is unlike pity, another result of sympathy, because whereas an empathic moment may indeed have a component of compassion, pity is not a usual response because when one is involved in empathizing, there is an understanding that surpasses pity. To feel pity means that someone may feel sorry for the distress of another, but does not actually feel the distress or pain of another.

And, of course, empathy is the exact opposite of apathy. Apathy says "I don't care at all," or "I couldn't care less," while empathy says, "I feel your pain and want to help alleviate it."

The ability to empathize may also help with the abilities of intuition and telepathy by establishing a connection with another person. In this, one would become aware of another person's distress and utilize the ability of intuition to discern the exact nature of the person's state. For example, there may be a feeling of discomfort emanating from the other person. By using intuition, an aspect of which includes the ability to perceive information about another person through the mutual connection to the interconnected web, you can pinpoint the cause for the discomfort. In the case of someone at a distance, such as one involved in an accident or other physical crisis, the empathic ability to sense another's pain and then send healing to that person can serve to effect a release of the pain, or at least help to alleviate it somewhat. While the healing is being sent, you can also utilize your telepathic abilities by sending thoughts of calm and peace, which will also help to lessen the person's distress.

Empathy is only possible because we really are connected through our spirits via the interdependent web. In other words, we are to take care of each other, despite not recognizing (all the time) the true nature of our being. In the body, we can entertain each other, knowing that we are all spirit. If we allow ourselves to acknowledge this truth, then it is an absolute reality and necessity that we intimately respond to each other's needs. By intimate, I mean the concept of a connection beyond the surface one we exhibit daily. While we need to keep each other separate in order to enjoy our unique experience of this plane, we also at the same time need to recognize the underlying connection we have to each other. This recognition in turn will help us to overcome our petty (or even large) differences.

By practicing an empathic connection with each other, we can allow ourselves to grow the spiritual connection that is our legacy from our previous existence on other planes. By developing and practicing empathy, you will learn to bring forth into the world a higher, more productive reality. This desire and ability to connect with each other in this way, and by extension with other non-incarnate spirits and higher entities, as well as the earth itself, is actually one of the reasons for the development of organized religions. There is a need to connect spiritually with each other, as well as to a higher being.

Practicing empathy can also be seen as a way of developing or enhancing telepathic ability. How do we practice empathy? It's easier than you may think. One exercise involves going to a location where a variety of people might be gathered, such as the central court of a mall or a busy restaurant. Sit quietly with your journal and allow yourself to relax. Take a few deep breaths. Select a person sitting across the way. Do not stare at this person, as that will make him or her uncomfortable. Simply know that this is the person you are going to connect with, then imagine your spirit reaching out to his or her spirit. Try to recognize the essence of you recognizing the essence of that person. You are not trying to be intrusive; you are simply trying to connect on a spiritual level with this other spirit sitting across from you. Remember, you are not having a stare-down contest with this person. He or she should not be aware that you are reaching out to them unless, of course, they, too, are trying to connect spiritually with another, and then the connection might be quite immediate and deep . . . connecting with another spirit is a joy-filled and exhilarating experience.

Now, as you reach out to this other person, focus your awareness both on your spirit and this other person's spirit. You will become aware of a sensation of warmth and perhaps a slight vibration. This sensation will most likely be detected in the area between your solar plexus and your heart. This is the area of the chakras associated with gut instincts, intuition, love, and compassion, and it is on this level of love that you are actually communicating with this other person, even if that other person's physical being is not aware of such communication. When you detect that glimmer of love growing within you, then you will be experiencing the bond associated with two spirits interacting. This is not the love of romance novels, but rather a more spiritual love. It is a part of the sensation of oneness with the world around you, with the spirit plane, with the universe.

Detecting a vibration in this part of your body is verification that you are perceiving and connecting with the spirit of another person. It may take a few tries (or trying with different people) to achieve this awareness, but once the connection is made, it is an unmistakable sensation. This exercise will help you not only to connect spiritually with another, but will allow you to become more aware of and more familiar with your own spirit and its reality. Once you feel comfortable working with your spirit being, and acknowledge its abilities, you can try to send forth a wave of love to those around you. You will be quite surprised to detect a wave of love coming back at you. Even those around you who are not aware of their own spirits, or are not familiar with utilizing this part of themselves, contain that essence that is well-aware that another spirit is reaching out toward them with love, and they will respond with a vibration of love sent back to you.

This interaction between spirits is also the basis of empathy. The conscious utilization of this ability to reach out to another will help to develop the oneness that is our legacy. On a more mundane level, we can use this ability to empathize, to feel another's state of being or state of mind, in order to understand the other person's motivation for acting in a certain manner. For example, when the person in the car behind us on the expressway suddenly veers around us and cuts us off, instead of feeling angry (road rage), you can next time mentally ask that person why they would do such a thing . . . what is their life like that they need to wield this kind of aggressive action and power on those around him or her. Try to really sense an answer, and since there is no way to verify that answer, you can create an appropriate one and send that person love from your spirit. Do I do this every time? My children would say no, but I try to meet the bad behavior of other drivers with a sense of love and understanding as much as I humanly (operative word here) can. If I were a perfected spirit, I wouldn't be driving a car.

Another way to practice empathy, on perhaps a more mundane level, is to practice Random Acts of Kindness. The phrase, "Practice random kindness and senseless acts of beauty" was first expressed by writer Anne Herbert in the early 1980s. RAKs are simply little actions one can take to ease another's steps on their path. This can involve something as simple as paying for the coffee of someone behind you in line or helping a neighbor with their snow shoveling. At the far end of kindness, it can involve signing your organ donor card, or donating a kidney. While this last is probably the hardest for most people, connecting to others through acts of kindness can not only help to brighten that person's day, but also increase the empathic love bonds across the interdependent web.

When I was teaching college English, one of the assignments I would give involved the students performing random acts of kindness and then writing an essay about what they did, how the person they did it for reacted, and how they felt performing the act and subsequently. In many cases, students were surprised by the transformative nature of the exercise, both for themselves and those they had helped.

Albert Einstein said,

> A human being is part of the whole that we call the universe, a part limited in time and space. He experiences himself, his thoughts and feelings, as something separated from the rest—a kind of optical illusion of consciousness. The illusion is a prison for us, restricting us to our personal desires and to affection for only the few people nearest us. Our task must be to free ourselves from this prison by widening our circle of compassion to embrace all living beings and all of nature.

The need to nurture universal empathy should be obvious. If we are feeling the pain of another, I believe we would be reluctant to inflict pain on another. The fundamental problem with humanity is that not everyone is able to feel compassion or the need for empathy. We have a need to categorize and separate in order to deal with the vast numbers of people, places, and events we become aware of each day. At its worst, this is an us-versus-them mentality. This separation is useful in understanding time or place, but not so very conducive to peace and harmony when applied to people. It is much easier to attack someone or some country when we do not intimately identify ourselves with them or recognize our common spiritual being.

Part of this is a misguided sense of self-preservation . . . if we open ourselves up (we believe), the other person is definitely going to attack some portion of our being. If, instead, we allow ourselves to practice empathy and really reach out to others, this fear of the other will dissipate like morning fog.

Empathy can help to govern morality and ethics because as one understands the emotional and physical distress (or wellbeing) of another, one will adjust one's behavior toward others in order to avoid inflicting distress or to encourage wellbeing. It would be hoped that all children could experience the effects of someone empathizing with their distress from a very young age, and thus learn how good it feels to have someone care about them and then, in turn, develop the ability to do the same for others. Sadly, some children never experience that caring and do not develop a healthy ability to empathize with others. This may explain the frustrations of child and teen bullies and others acting out violently because they lacked being nurtured, which is necessary to being able to nurture and relate to others.

Children need to be taught empathy, if not at home, then in school, where training can take place to teach the perceptions and reactions inherent in the act of empathy, if not in a psychic manner, at least on the physical plane. This training can involve role-playing activities that will stimulate the empathic response. A more empathic society will be a kinder, gentler one.

As was discussed in Chapter 1, my ability to perceive the pain of Martha having had her braces tightened is really akin to empathy, especially in the sense of not only perceiving her pain, but then taking that pain into my own body in order to give her some relief. While this is a well-thought out summation of the occurrence, at the time it was a more nebulous awareness. At the time, I just accepted it, and only later was I able to think through the ramifications of this event.

Since then, I have had many more moments of such awareness, where the pain of another, known or unknown to me, seemed to enter my awareness and/or, unbidden, my body. I have become more adept at holding the pain at arm's length. Physical empathic manifestation is stressful on the body and while it is sometimes necessary to take the burden of another on the physical level, for the most part it is just as beneficial to perceive the existence of the distress (be it physical, mental, or emotional) and send healing. This can be even more of a relief for the person whose pain one is sensing than would be the physical taking on of the pain.

The idea of empathizing with those about to enter into a non-physical existence, or whose physical connection is tenuous, is not as remote as you might think. When we hear of someone close to death, we can perceive his or her distress, if that is what he or she is feeling, or his or her fear. We send thoughts (or prayers) of wellbeing and peace. We hope for a speedy recovery or a peaceful transition. We might think towards the person words of healing, hope, and encouragement. All of this falls under the category of the gift of empathy.

When my son Alex was a sophomore in high school, a classmate of his was in a terrible accident one night. Two of the other passengers died at the scene, two others were injured, and my son's classmate was on the cusp of life and transitioning for a week. I had never met the boy and knew nothing about him, but I felt drawn to send him thoughts of healing and encouragement. When we first "connected," he was lying in a hospital bed and I was in my home. I told him not to be afraid, because I sensed he was tremendously so, and I asked him about himself, and suddenly, I could see him next to me, in baseball uniform, tossing a baseball into the air. Now, remember, I knew nothing about him at this point, and news reports had only dealt with the details of the accident, and those who had immediately transitioned and not so much with details about the individuals who were still living.

I mentioned this detail to my son. Although he wasn't close to the boy, his best friend was, and he told me that the boy loved baseball more than anything and played on the school's team. I took this as a definite confirmation that I was in contact with Teddy.

As the week went by, I spent time each day letting Teddy know he wasn't alone. At some point, I came to understand that the time was near for him to transition, so I told him to look around for relatives who had died and that they would help him. He indicated he had seen people he knew were no longer alive. I told him this was good and to not be afraid. About a week after the accident, I was resting on my couch in front of the TV, but with my back to it. Suddenly I felt compelled to turn over. At that moment, I saw a cloud of swirling grey smoke spiraling towards the ceiling. In the instant, I knew Teddy had transitioned, and I wished him well. A little while later, the news report came on that confirmed that Teddy had passed on earlier. I knew he had taken the time to see those closest to him and then had kindly come to me.

So, you see, we can also empathize with those we can only know in spirit, and offer comfort, healing, solace, and guidance.

Empathy puts into play all of our paranormal senses and marking a differentiation between these is as ludicrous as doing so for our physical senses. Do we think: I am hearing this music with my ears and my sense of touch is detecting a cold breeze across my neck as my taste buds are being satisfied by this juicy strawberry. No! Nor do we think: I am perceiving that person's joy clairaudibly or clairsentiently. We sense another's state by simply detecting a ripple within the web that declares, "I am in pain" or "I am joyous" without much thought of the means of that perception.

Sometimes, we can meet someone and take an instant like or dislike to them, through no overt communication of their internal state, or some indicator that we should like them or not. In the same way, we can reach out to someone in empathy and find a cesspool of negative energy. I do not mean to be unkind, but there are beings incarnate who, most often through conscious choice, have decided to adopt the negative vibrational patterns of lower, less evolved entities. When you detect these beings, the best thing to do is NOT to empathize, for there is nothing that you will be able to do, as their state is really their choice (made before or after incarnating), and theirs are energies you should not involve yourself with, let alone touch. It is far better to send out a love vibration, and let those people go from your thoughts.

By now, it should be apparent that all of the "paranormal" abilities and activities with which this book deals are all interconnected and are indeed different aspects of the same gifts utilized to perceive the same energy, albeit in different forms and seemingly from various sources. If we keep in mind the truth that we are all essentially spirit connected together within one framework of reality, despite the illusion of time and space differentials, it is easier to understand how empathy, intuition, telepathy, clairvoyance, etc. work and how these are useful tools in communication, compassion, and camaraderie. These ideas are not new or unique, but rather are a part of our human legacy.

Empathy encourages us to truly reach out to people, to get to know them and truly feel their joy and their pain. This responsibility also encourages us to instigate or share in the joy and help to ease or alleviate the pain.

In a 1968 episode of *Star Trek* entitled "The Empath," crew members are held on a planet and subjected to physical harm in order to teach Gem, an empath, not to fear her natural impulse to heal them through empathy. The cruelty shown by the planet's rulers is in direct juxtaposition to the virtue they are trying to develop in Gem.

Are our planet's rulers also oblivious to the fundamental cause of so many natural and man-made disasters afflicting our world? Does the modern sense of disconnection (from each other) create the situation of mass violence and killing? Does this sense allow strangers to kill each other? Is it the reason for overwhelming selfish behavior, as seen locally on the level of road rage, and globally with the disregard for the environment and the wellbeing of the planet? If we are not actually interacting with each other and with the planet as a whole, how do we develop a sense of responsibility for the next person, and for the planet he or she is living on? If we were all able to practice empathy, we would be more fully aware of the worldwide unity in spirit and seek the means to heal each other, and the planet.

Chapter 9

The Gift of Discernment:
Forays into Religion

There is no need for temples, no need for complicated philosophies. My brain and my heart are my temples; my philosophy is kindness.
(The Dalai Lama)

All religions are reflections of the culture, philosophies, and economics of a certain people in a certain place at a certain time. Religion helps to explain the natural world, creates community in which to interact with that natural world, and, in most cases, offers a means to attempt to control the natural world, be it the nature rituals of native Americans, the veneration of the ancestors in Shinto, or the required rites of the Roman Catholic church. Whether to influence the immediate aspects of nature (making it rain, beseeching the higher being for aid), or the future aspect of the natural world (ensuring a place in Heaven, avoiding hell), religion exists to help incarnate people with the illusion that they can somehow control their physical world. What does not seem to be understood is that events and occurrences will happen independently of the performed rituals. If a Wiccan, for example, does a ritual to attract love, and that love does not appear, it is not necessarily the failure of the ritual, but perhaps the timing was not acceptable to the larger interdependent web that may be holding a larger sway here.

Marx said that "religion is the opiate of the masses." What does this mean? Does he mean in the same way vision drugs (peyote, etc.) are employed to enhance religious experience? Hardly . . . it means that religion, which has the possibility of bringing people together for the better good and for mutual growth and enlightenment, instead often tends to mystify the spiritual in favor of the truly mundane. It means that many religions, especially those that rely on fundamentalist fervor to retain their members, offer modes of altered states of consciousness in order to keep the masses under control and to entice them to stay loyal and keep coming. Perhaps there isn't an actual intake of drugs, but often (and I am referring to those sects requiring strict obedience) the chanting, praying, whirling, etc., can lead to a state of consciousness that offers the appearance of connection with the higher being, while really it is a natural high meant to seduce and control.

While the result of religion is often to build community (of one sort or another), the main purpose is to address the fear of death and to establish rules of behavior (morality and ethics). Personally, I would like to think that religion should be a place where people come together to potluck, bring their own real and figurative dishes to the table, and eat and talk together in a communal setting. No judgment, no holier-than-thou-ness, just a time to share the light (and, of course, the food). Unfortunately, many times religion leads to using the fear of death as a means of controlling the community and getting others to opt in.

In addition, religion can serve to set up an us vs. them mentality: my religion is better, more correct, more real than yours and thus it is the supreme religion and the only one everyone should be a member of. This thinking is most often found in fundamentalist religions, but even moderates of different sects have been known to disagree (sometimes vehemently and violently) with each other.

There is a marked difference between being religious and being spiritual, although one does not necessarily preclude the other. One can be in a religion and still recognize the spirit within oneself and within others; however, a spiritual person does not need to be in an organized religion in order to commune with their own spirit or the spirits of others, as this book has spent some time pointing out. A spiritual person recognizes that theirs is an infinite community, rather than a finite one. There are other spirits incarnate, and there are spirits disincarnate. It is a large community within which the truly spiritual can chose to live (and do live, in fact).

Of course, there will be those who believe that the true purpose of religion is to worship God. But that God is as variously defined and envisioned as there are religions. The old man with white hair and a beard, sitting on a throne in heaven, with a book of judgmental notations is only one way of envisioning God. There may be a god with many arms, or many faces. God might not have a discernable shape; and of course there are those who do not believe in God because they cannot see him (or her).

The spiritual person, who recognizes spirit in him/herself and others and nature, etc., will come to understand that God is as infinite as we are. I am not saying that, as individuals, we are god, but I am suggesting that the combination of all things of spirit, taken together and blended as the scrambled eggs of my childhood paradigm, may be the closest thing to the real essence of god. Still creative and creating, still loving and kind, god is the full and total expression of the spiritual, which ends up being everything eternal.

We are not unlike caterpillars, measuring our small piece of earth, and then, after an intermediate stage of rest, transforming/transitioning into butterflies who are able to escape the confines of this limited plane and fly up to a wider, freer, and, perhaps, more expressive one. In this place, after transitioning, once our vision is not obscured by being incarcerated in a physical body, we are able to see clearly. Enlightened beings, Masters who have incarnated, have a wider range/field of vision than the average incarnate spirit. Thus, they are able to relate to us what it is they are perceiving, but, given the limitations of language, these descriptions are often embedded in "better than here, wonderful, awesome" terms because while it seems, from the discarnate people I have spoken to, there is more a sense of freedom and clarity there, life pretty much goes on . . . i.e., no one has ever mentioned any sort of angel type work, no harp quartets, etc. Additionally, no one I have ever spoken to has ever made mention of religious dogma or differences. Whatever disagreements we have here, these do not seem to continue on the other side. The only time religion has come up, it has been through observation, as in the case mentioned earlier of the discarnate woman so committed to her beliefs, she is unable to open her eyes and see what is around her.

On a recent episode of a popular talk show, a guest said, with great authority, that spirituality is a longing. I am not sure what that might mean, but from my view, spirituality is the realization that we are all spirit and, therefore, we are all one, capable of living peaceful and productive lives together. While there might be, indeed, a longing to become more spiritual or to further understand one's own spiritual existence and how that existence combines with that which others are experiencing, spirituality is not the longing for an answer, it is the answer. Once we realize our spiritual essence, we can put aside our petty and earth-based differences and evolve to the next standard of existence.

No discarnate spirit has ever said anything about religion to me, though the effects of the impact of over-zealous religion can easily be witnessed. There are spirits who, once they reach the other side of the veil, seem trapped in their own mythologies, most of which are impressed upon them by the leaders of fear-based religions.

Another sitter has a grandmother in spirit who is surrounded by yellow light, beautiful radiating beams, but she is stuck on her knees, praying at what appears to be a communion railing, waiting for Jesus to come to her. In the meantime, relatives and friends in spirit are trying to get her attention, but to no avail. She is absolutely blinded to her new reality, and instead is clinging to the mythologies that have brainwashed her into thinking she has to wait for Jesus to lead her to the promised land, or heaven.

Once, when I was visiting Lily Dale, I saw a t-shirt that read, "Religion is for people afraid of going to hell. Spirituality is for people who have already been there."

Additionally, and perhaps most importantly, hell is seen as a place where one is separated from the sought after deity. The fear of being consigned to hell and, thus, being separated from the deity is the factor most religions use in order to maintain control over the masses. If you "sin," you go to hell, which means you had better work overtime being good in order to avoid that fate. The two spirits mentioned earlier who seem stuck in an unproductive state of denial might be considered to be living in a sort of hell, though perhaps the idea of purgatory is more appropriate: a place of neither goodness nor badness, but where one can eventually come to their new conscious state. When spirit transitions from this dimension to the next, the hope is for no more discomfort or disorientation than one would find passing through a door, or, as spiritualists say, a veil. Yet, if one has been so indoctrinated as to believe in more than this simple process, a hell or purgatory is created for them by them. They create the reality they believe to be true, whether it is in fact true or not. Thus, the woman kneeling by the communion rail may feel at peace, waiting for Jesus, but in fact, physical knees or not, she is going to eventually get tired of remaining in that position and move on, finally hearing those around her who are calling for her to join them.

Islam, Judaism, and Christianity, which are primarily the same doctrines employing different expressions, speak of love and compassion. In their fundamentalist form, however, these religions seem to thrive on hating the other two through a well-developed arrogance and superiority. People do not usually go to war over the preference for classical versus modern art, a Michelangelo versus a Klee, a da Vinci versus a Van Gogh, but they do go to war over religion. Both ideas, though, are equally absurd. Just as art captures and interprets the world and ideas around us through the eyes of the artists, so, too, does religion. The founders of any religion looked at the same world, the same universe, and tried to explain what they saw and developed methods for living within that perceived reality. Religions, like works of art, are no more or less expressions of the same thing.

One Sunday morning, as I drove with my father to get the weekly brunch fare of bagels and lox, I asked him what he thought God was. He reached over and turned up the radio, from which was emanating the melodious sounds of some classical piece of music. "That is God," he said. He didn't elaborate on this and instead pulled into the parking spot in front of the store and opened his door. Dad had been a philosophy major at Harvard, but this is one lesson I do not think he learned there, but rather from his life experiences. God was that thing that was both creator and created. It was the beauty around us that was natural and that which was man-made.

For better or worse, I was born into a Jewish family, whose branches included atheists, agnostics, and the devout. My family always referred to me as a stomach Jew, because while there was, for me, an intense lack of spiritual content in the religion (as is true of most western religions), there was a certain amount of foods and cultural elements that created something recognizable as a shared community experience. Sunday School consisted of learning the history of the Jews, which was seemingly endless, and also not particularly accurate, since when we moved to Rochester and from the reform temple of Schenectady to (briefly) a conservative one, and the Rabbi asked me who the first man was, I confidently answered "Adam," which was, in this building, incorrect. "The first man was Abraham," the Rabbi chided me.

I never felt close to Judaism. The brand we were affiliated with, reform, didn't really address the God issue, and seemed to lack a spiritual core. Also, there weren't too many rituals that were all that interesting to a child. My Catholic friends across the street in Schenectady seemed to have rituals pouring from their pores. Theirs was a large family, so someone was always having First Communion, with the pretty white dress and veil, or going to catechism, or going to the beautiful church around the corner. And they told me of mystical occurrences, for example how every year on Good Friday at noon the skies would darken and it would start to rain in honor of Jesus' death. And, by God, at least that year, the skies darkened at noon and it began to rain (after that I often forgot to note the weather on Good Friday).

One Sunday, they invited me to join them at Mass, and I happily snuck out of the house and joined them. Oh, my, there certainly was enough going on to keep a young person entertained . . . candles and incense, and priests in beautiful robes, and people standing and kneeling, and then walking forward to receive communion. I wanted to experience communion, too, but was told I couldn't because of some preparation for it that I did not have. Years later, I would sneak up to the communion rail at an Episcopalian church in Fredonia and the befuddled priest gave me the body and blood of Christ, which turned out to be matzo and wine, making me feel, on the one hand that I had done some sort of evil act by taking communion, and then, on the other hand, realizing that it felt like I had "regressed" back to Seder mode.

When I lived in Washington, D.C., I would go to midnight Mass at St. Matthew's, across the street from where I worked. At midnight, everyone went silent and the bells rang to welcome the newborn child. That was an awe-inspiring moment, but still not enough to make me want to join this highly regulated religion.

In addition to my involvement in Judaism and Christianity, I have also studied and to some extent practiced aspects of Buddhism and Spiritualism, both of which inform my current belief system and practice, but neither of which seems able to simplify the reality of spiritual existence enough for me to embrace these in their entirety.

Yet, if one approaches religion and ritual in the spirit (double entendre intended) of working with the universe for the greater good of all and the highest expression of the individual within that oneness, it can be a worthy endeavor and far more fulfilling than approaching it from a state of fear and anxiety. It is this impetus that has drawn me back to the nature-based practices, much like my communing in my backyard as a small child with the heightened vibrance and vibrations of the natural world around me.

Clearing a sheet of tattered newspaper from the branches of a readying-itself-to-bloom forsythia is just as much an act of reverence and respect as kneeling in a pew, and there is a sense of immediacy that is hard to beat in the former. In this act, I feel a connection not only to this forsythia, but to nature itself, and thus to the creator and the creation.

Since so much of religion is based on humankind's fear of death, I hope, in offering proof of survival of this transition, that some will find a modicum of comfort and perhaps start to live lives filled with hope and joy, rather than fear and blind obedience to dogma.

Chapter 10

The Gift of Community:
Building Spiritual Community

*Be the change that you want to see in the world.
(Mohandas Gandhi)*

We are all petals in the cosmic lotus blossom, unfolding together. Once we really look at ourselves—under the superficial color of skin, type of hair, where we live—and start focusing on our universally alike spirit selves, then we will start to feel a personal responsibility, one for the other. The Hollywood people working on African issues can see this because they have dealt with surface and know it is fleeting. They are in artist's head, which admits the existence of spirit for its survival. One needs a healthily developed imagination and creative spirit to see that eternal spirit that is connected one to the other, through the interdependent web. The physical may be beautiful, but it is definitely fragile and perishable. You can't scratch spirit—it resists not necessarily change, but, rather, modification. It is, we are, one and the same. We are responsible to the spirit in ourselves, and responsible for the spirit connection and oneness with each other. Then we become responsible for their fragile skin and the housing of that spirit, in the spirit of Namaste, which means my spirit bows to your spirit.

> Namaste—the hands come together at heart and/or forehead level. A bow, and the sacred sound is pronounced, the sacred salutation: the divine spark in me bows to the divine spark in you.
>
> Namaste (nah-mah-stay) equalizes those coming together—king and peasant contain the

same divinity. Both are made of the same energy. Each inhabits a body, is impelled to a life path, completes the journey, and then lays aside the shell to become pure spirit once again.

Namaste—we are the same, deep down and high above, we share a common source, no matter our station in life, or our outlook, or ideology. Shadowed by the vagaries of life, we become separate from the commonalities of our true nature. We lose our sense of being in relationship, one with the other and, in doing so, find and amplify our differences and use these to create me-versus-you, us-versus-them scenarios that lead to more divisive actions, fist fights, and sword fights, and bombings and wars.

Namaste—I bow to you, you bow to me. We recognize our alikeness and, in that recognition, rise above our differences. We are at peace because we are part of the same thing . . . my right hand will not inflict pain on my left hand. You are familiar, a long lost sibling in the light that is our true selves.

Namaste—it is no unplanned coincidence that we are encouraged to love God (by whatever name we know that being) with all our heart and soul and mind and, in the next breath, to love our neighbor as ourselves. Each is the same . . . as the vessel of the divine spark, we must love each other and in doing so, we love God. When we love God, we are loving the divine spark in each other.

Namaste—we will not let our differences in shading or creed or nationality or political persuasion or economic status or religious or sexual orientation keep us from acknowledging our sameness, our oneness in the universe. The small starving child in Niger is my sibling in the light and I have a duty and obligation to ease her hardship. The person whose hatred of those not like him colors his thoughts and determines his actions is my sibling in the light, and it is my obligation to bow to his divine spark in hopes that he becomes aware of it in himself and, in doing so, learns to bow to that spark in another.

Namaste—the Jew and the Catholic and the Christian and the Muslim and the Buddhist and the Hindu and the Shaman and the Pagan all contain the same spark, are of the same origin. Their religions cannot, must not mitigate the reality of this truth. Temple, church, mosque, or hillside . . . the differences in the physical structure of their places of worship do not alter the common spark within their separate physical bodies.

Namaste—I wear purple or green or blue. I eat chicken or beef or tofu. Outward appearances do not alter the light shining within me and within you. We are siblings in the light. Does this seem simplistic? Sure, of course! Sometimes the real answers, the true answers are preposterously simple. If who we really are, our essence, is made of the same stuff, the same expression of a larger whole, then where is the sense in fighting with each other, in killing each other? Disagreements? Sure . . . siblings argue, sometimes they fight, but in trying to discern our common spiritual origin, wouldn't we also find our common earthly expression? And in doing this, do we then not strive to heal whatever separates our shining lights, one from the other? A fire provides greater light, greater warmth, and produces greater useable energy when it is whole, rather than divided into separate flames.

Namaste—the divine spark in me bows to the divine spark in you. In our most basic state, we are the same. Let our spiritual familiarity overcome our human frailties. Let each spark contribute to rather than detract from the life-sustaining fire of our shared experience on earth. Namaste . . . .

We have gone from the spirituality of the past to the current non-spiritual era and we will cycle back to a more spiritual existence in the future. Religions have distanced themselves from nature over the last 200 years as we have moved from an agrarian to industrial-based world. We have lost contact with nature entities.

Those who helped to bring about the Industrial Revolution had a different paradigm. They did not see the aspects of the earth as one entity, dependent on each other for survival, but as separate entities and the "parts interacted with each other as part of a machine rather than parts of a living organism. The earth was there as a resource for humans, a 'collection of objects not a communion of subjects'" (Thomas Berry).

It is, however, the earlier paradigm that fostered an understanding that humanity's relationship with the ecosystem is one of being part of it rather than a manipulator of it and that this awareness is imperative for the survival of the planet. Understanding that the demise of a species or the desecration of a body of water, for example, has a negative impact on the survival of humankind is becoming ever more vital. Thus care must be taken to consciously wed ourselves to the ecosystem and remember and recognize our interactive role in it. This is known as eco-spiritualism.

"It is time for a paradigm shift about how we feel about and deal with the planet. It is important to acknowledge that the earth is not just for our exploitation of it, but that we are a part of it," said Clare Danielsson, who transitioned on 2/8/07 and was the Steward of Boughton Place, an Eco-Spiritual Center for Re-Inhabiting the Earth in Highland, New York.

Clare Danielsson believed that we are to "look after your least by creating a society of systematic unselfishness.... People who have things need to learn to give and people who need things need to learn how to receive. Thus will each be responsible for and to the other and all will help to create a caring and loving community."

Her ideal was to "put love into a world where you don't see it much. We are responsible for each other and this responsibility should not be left to the state or the church. It is in reality and in practice, an individual responsibility."

Clare gathered people around her at Boughton Place, an eco-spiritual center for re-inhabiting the earth. According to its mission statement, based on the philosophy of Thomas Berry, it serves those who are interested in "carrying out the transition from a period of human devestation of the Earth to a period when humans would be present to the planet in a beneficial manner."

On a positive note, most religions have some form of what is known in the west as the Golden Rule. "Every religion emphasizes human improvement, love, respect for others, sharing other people's suffering. On these lines every religion had more or less the same viewpoint and the same goal" (The Dalai Lama).

The concept and practice of empathy can also be seen as closely related to the Golden Rule, which is such a very important precept that it appears in all cultures and religions in one form or another. "Do unto other as you would have them do unto you," can also be written "No one of you is a believer until he desires for his brother that which he desires for himself," (Islam) and "Regard your neighbor's gain as your gain, and your neighbor's loss as your own loss," (Taoism). The understanding here regarding empathy is that the pain of another is something you should not inflict, but rather alleviate, lest you be the unfortunate recipient of such pain.

These golden rules remind us to take into account the existence of another as our responsibility, that we are, indeed, responsible each for the other. It is the same concept as the Indian adage that to truly understand another, you must walk a mile in his (or her) shoes, and thus be able to understand more intimately their existence and their perception of reality.

The Harmonic Convergence took place August 16 and 17, 1987. The event was based on the research of José Arguellas an artist and student of the Mayan culture and calendar, who believed that certain aspects of this calendar, i.e., those of a prophetic nature, seemed to be imminent. Not only did the calendar seem to predict the Harmonic Convergence, but it also indicates that a global shift will occur on December 21, 2012, at 11:11

GMT, which will result in a new, more enlightened age on earth.

The Harmonic Convergence involved the physical alignment of planets in our solar system and this alignment was to have helped to focus energies on earth that would combine through the acts of meditation and prayer to foster a new age of love, peace, and hope. It was when there was to be an alignment of psychic and cosmic forces in order to bring about change in the long-established patterns of earth. Many people from around the world gathered together, or spent time alone, waiting for the moment of alignment in order to channel that energy and combine it with those around the planet in hopes of refocusing humankind's intention and creating a new more empathic and nurturing paradigm for our existence in the interdependent web, bringing into realization the true interdependence of our reality.

While certain events did occur subsequently that seemed to usher in a more peaceful and cooperative era, such as the breakup of the Soviet Union, the destruction of the Berlin Wall, which led to the re-unification of Germany, and the end of Apartheid in South Africa, many conflicts and disasters continued and began, including civil wars, genocides, famines, the catastrophic events of 9/11, and the war and loss of lives in Iraq and Afghanistan. In addition, today we are facing the prospect of global warming and the degradation of our environment and depletion of the natural resources necessary to sustain life on earth.

The impact of such global efforts as the Harmonic Convergence cannot be minimized. The convergence created a harmonic vibration that permeated the planet and all who lived upon her and served to underscore the need to shift from a physical/materialistic focus to a spiritual/psychic focus for humanity, resulting in a transformation leading to cooperation and an end of conflict.

Unfortunately, but predictably, there is much resistance to this sort of paradigm shift. There are those who called this event the "Moronic Convergence" and yet, these same people gather together weekly in houses of worship, often praying for this or that event to occur, from healing to peace. There is, indeed, a positive, powerful energy created by a group meditating on love and peace. However, not all members have to be in the same place.

I believe the 11:11 phenomenon offers us all daily opportunities to join with others from around the world, or at least in our own time zone, in a moment of focus on positive affirming of a higher, more enlightened reality.

Have you ever walked into a room, looked at the clock and read the number "11:11?" Does the time or number 11:11 seem to be cropping up more frequently in your life? Has the increased awareness of this number made you wonder whether it is merely a coincidence or if there is some meaning, some purpose to this repeated appearance?

More and more people around the world are becoming aware of the 11:11 phenomenon, as it is widely referred to, and theories abound about what it could mean. The consensus seems to be that whatever its precise meaning, the message it is bringing is a positive one.

Many theories center on the notion that the world is currently being repeatedly battered and thrown into states of darkness. Starting with the assassinations of John F. Kennedy, Robert F. Kennedy, and Martin Luther King, Jr., and continuing through 9/11 and the multitude of acts of terrorism and other violent incidents, the world is experiencing an increase in human violence against itself. In addition, it is believed that the worldwide environment is echoing this negative energy, especially as seen in the recent dramatic increase in natural disasters including the Southeast Asian Tsunami and the amazingly high number of hurricanes and tornadoes in recent seasons.

It is believed, among those who are given to experiencing and thinking about such things, that the 11:11 phenomenon is a communication from another dimension, from individuals in another state of being—spirits, angels—to help those so touched (and the numbers are increasing daily) to remember and be aware of a greater purpose, a more positively-filled energy that can be drawn upon by humankind.

It is the general consensus that this positive energy is contained in light, which is being sent to earth, in part through this phenomenon, to dispel the darkness. And within this light are the seeds of love and peace. In fact, people who experience this phenomenon are sometimes referred to as Lightworkers, especially those people who respond actively to the 11:11 call to take a moment and contemplate more spiritually uplifting possibilities for this world. Pausing for a minute to think of love and peace seems such a small thing to do in one's busy schedule, but the idea of many people thinking the same thoughts at the same moment, and perhaps having an impact on the world, is truly an amazing one.

Those called to join in with the 11:11 meditation often focus on what is known as the Metta Prayer: "May all beings be happy, may all beings be peaceful, may all beings be safe. May all beings awaken to the light of their true nature. May all beings be free."

Interestingly, when one person tells another about this phenomenon, the second person often begins to have the same experience. Just recently, I was speaking with a friend about this and when she got into her car, the clock read 1:11 (considered a related number). The next day, she happened to look up at the clock at the moment when it read 11:11, and a woman who had overheard our first conversation told us that she, too, had begun to see the number 11:11 without any effort on her part. It is not as though these women, and many other people, are consciously making the effort to watch the clock. One of the stranger (more miraculous?) aspects of this phenomenon is that it just happens without any prior intention.

In the meantime, other "coincidences" occurred as I wrote this piece. I happened upon a car, the license plate of which was composed entirely of the number "1." As I was writing just now, it suddenly occurred to me that a pertinent passage from the Bible also incorporates this number: Hebrews 11:1 reads "Now, faith is being sure of what we hope for and certain of what we do not see." It would seem that for those experiencing this phenomenon, faith is a major component in accepting this calling to pay attention to something higher, wider, and more light-filled than oneself.

It is also interesting to note the "coincidence" of Armistice Day. Peace was signed back into existence in 1918 on the 11th day of the 11th month at the 11th hour, at which time all major hostilities comprising World War I ceased.

As I wrote these last few lines, I "happened" to look at the clock . . . you guessed it: 11:11.

Whether these messages are from other-plane beings or not would be hard to prove with sufficient evidence to satisfy the criticisms and inquiries of the naysayers. But, the positive nature of the experience is hard to refute. For thousands in a time zone to become aware simultaneously of the number 11:11 and to stop to think about the light of love and peace might just be the necessary action that will begin to eradicate the darkness and usher in a new era on earth.

If all religions serve to coordinate communication with the creator/divinity and explain the world/universe around us, then earth-based/earth aware/bio-reverent spiritual awareness, with or without rituals, would serve as well, if not far better than traditional western religious expression.

Our intrinsic nature, as primarily spiritual beings, allows us to easily commune with nature and each other. As spirit permeates everything, our spirit can enter into partnership both with the spirit incarnate and the spirit of the tree, the flower, the frog, the cat. We are one in our real selves with the all, with the one. No way but through me could be no way but with me— an enlightened one showing the way of oneness—we are all together the spiritual essence of the universe.

And, as we hustle and bustle from one place to another, from work, to home, to driving children from one place to another, we lose touch with the very space we are moving through as we do so. No longer are we outside to be outside. Our children no longer spend time in backyards and parks. Their lives, too, have become over-filled with a long to-do list. We are no longer experiencing nature and being a part of nature. That part of our spirituality that echoes spiritual reality has become more difficult to identify in ourselves. This feeling of being disconnected from our natural environment can also lead to feelings of disorientation, or being lost, and of being generally unhealthy. A walk in the park or sitting by moving water can go a long way in finding peace within oneself and reconnecting our spirit with the larger spirit, the world spirit around us.

It seems that the arts may be an expression of the spirit's need to create. Whether visual or performing art, there is at its inception the impulse to bring into being a fresh perspective on the world(s) around us. The realm of the imagination is the place where spirit meets fertile loam in which all is brought to fruition, be it the imagination of the individual, or the imagination of the larger existence (i.e., the web, or "god").

The artist looks, for example into the very being of the daffodil, and brings forth his/her particular understanding of that daffodil. The viewer of the artwork is able to discern the artist's moment with the essence of the daffodil. The artist, the creator's moment of involved understanding of the essence of another thing, living or not, is a moment of awareness of its, for lack of a better word, divinity. And that divinity is housed in the spirit that inhabits all, and connects all.

When I lie back on the grass and look into the sky, the same sky that rained down Shekinah goldenness upon me as a child, I feel the pulsating of the spirit deep within the earth, the heartbeat, so to speak, of a world that sustains me and of which I (and everyone) am an intrinsic part. We are all here now, because we are meant to all be here now. In our presence, our sheer existence in this apparent time/space (that is not <u>really</u>

a separate time/place) is vital—each part of the whole is vital for the realization, the actualization of the whole. If one spirit were to become lost from the path they have chosen to walk, then our world would be different—we might never know this difference in order to acknowledge it, but the oneness of which we are all a part would know and grieve the loss. That same oneness rejoices in our common experiences and individual expression. In striving to celebrate this oneness, by working to overcome divisive thoughts and behaviors, we actualize the potential that was inherent in the first spark of the creation by the creator that was/is us—ever creating, in love and peace—namaste!

About the author . . .

I have always seen the world differently than most people apparently do. I see and talk with spirits. I sense empathically the joys, sorrows and pains of others. I have been a conduit through which spirit has offered solace to the bereaved, hope to the hopeless, and guidance to the lost. I have used my intuition to avoid roadblocks and, when I have ignored it, I have run head-first into brick walls. As a psychic and a spiritual intuitive, I have proved to myself and others that there is more than what we can perceive with our five senses. And yet, each time I am able to contact a loved one who has passed over and given the bereaved factual and verifiable evidence of their survival, I am awed, and grateful that I am able to be of service to people on both sides of the veil.

Please visit tobiehewitt.wordpress.com, for more information and links.

Made in the USA
Charleston, SC
24 September 2012